FORBIDDEN FRUIT

Declan Henry

FORBIDDEN FRUIT

Life and Catholicism
in Contemporary Ireland

DECLAN HENRY

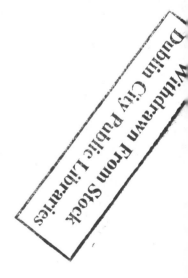

The
London
Press

Forbidden Fruit — First published by The London Press, UK 2020

ISBN: 978-1-907313-05-9

A C.I.P. reference is available from the British Library.

Dedicated to my brother Kevin

DISCLAIMER

I interviewed thirty priests for this book. In some cases, their names and certain other details have been changed to protect their identities and anonymity.

CONTENTS

A REFLECTION ON
FORBIDDEN FRUIT

Fr Joe McDonald

To speak the truth is a difficult task. To speak the truth in love is not only difficult but is, in my experience, rarely achieved. This is a hard hitting piece of work but it is not a tirade. Henry does not pull his punches, nor does he put the boot in — though if he had done, many would argue, with considerable justification, that it would be well deserved by the church.

This is a serious book about a serious topic, but it avoids harshness. I think one of its greatest strengths, which is also a key reason why it does not descend into mudslinging, is that the author also manages to avoid caricature. In so doing, and in his undertakings with real people, he acknowledges the complexity of much of the material under examination.

This is a special book and indeed a book of significance. It will prove an important text for many, and what might be surprising is how it will speak to many disparate groups. Three groups in particular come to mind. Firstly, given the book's title and subject matter, I expect the many people who have been hurt, and in a multiplicity of ways, will be drawn with little need of encouragement to read this book. They will not be disappointed. Another group, perhaps, will be those 'somewhere in the middle', who know next to nothing about how the church is internally, and indeed less about how the church made a right mess of things, especially in the area of sexuality. Neither will this group be disappointed. The third group I believe will be drawn to this book is the people who, despite all that has happened, simply have to, in varying degrees, hang on to their love for the church. Strange as it may seem nor will this group be disappointed. How can this be? How can a book written on such sensitive subject matter have such a broad appeal?

Precisely because this book is brave. It is considered, thought provoking and real. Perhaps it is the fact that the author interviewed over thirty priests and sought out salient aspects of their stories that lends its distinctively authentic hue.

This is a broader piece of work than one might initially expect. Yes, it unapologetically discusses the church and certainly does not shirk the many troublesome flashpoints, but it does so in the context of contemporary Ireland. Declan Henry's style is discursive and very engaging and I can honestly say if it was twice the size I would have been thrilled to invest in the time and effort of reading.

This book brings about clear rewards. I felt a number of times that it would serve as an excellent primer for all those engaging in the increasingly popular study of the survival of the church in a secular age — but it is much more. In fact we are taken on a journey akin to the Via Crucis, and experience the shame and degradation that was both the lot of the Crucified Saviour, and in recent times that of much of the contemporary church. However, in the words of the good thief 'in our case we deserved it', we are reminded of the fragility of our condition, and indeed the human aspects of being church.

When I turned the final page and closed the cover of *Forbidden Fruit* I felt a surge of hope.

This is fresh. It is real. In my own journey — which has taken me on a constant oscillation between righteous rage at, and passionate defence of the church — seldom have I encountered a voice like Henry's. Yes, he uses the scalpel and, yes, he lances and indeed treats several ecclesial maladies, but he does so with compassion. In wielding a scalpel with compassion, and speaking the truth in love, Declan Henry has done us some service, whether we are in the church, not sure any more, or long gone from it.

Henry's service also includes that he did not leave us atop Calvary Hill but, albeit tentatively, has dared to sketch the little chink of light breaking through on Easter morn.

FOREWORD

Fr. Bernárd Lynch

On reading Declan Henry's book I realise that one must travel very far, among saints with nothing to gain or outcasts with nothing to lose, to find a place where being Irish and Catholic does not matter. As we know we cannot escape our origins, however hard we try, those origins that contain the key — could we but find it — to all that we later become. It means something to me as a gay man and priest to have been born at a time in Ireland when the 'blessed trinity of Fianna Fáil, the GAA and the Catholic Church' reigned supreme. It is a sentimental error, therefore, to believe that the past is dead; it means nothing to say that it is all forgotten. Oedipus did not remember the thongs that bound his feet; nevertheless, the marks they left testified to that doom toward which his feet were leading him. The child may not remember the person who struck him, but the pain is forever etched in his soul.

Reading through this book, it seems to me that if we are to come to terms with our historically tortured Irish identity, then we have to hold in mind forever two ideas that seem to be in opposition. The first idea is acceptance. The acceptance, totally without rancour of the fact that I was, and millions like me were, for most of our lives, sexual outlaws in the land of our birth. No change in legislation could erase this indelible mark of alienation. In light of this idea, it goes without saying that injustice is commonplace. But this does not mean that we can ever, or have ever been, complacent. The second idea is of equal power: that one must never, in one's own life, accept injustices as commonplace but must fight them with all one's strength. This fight begins, however, in the heart and is laid to our charge that as soon as we set out on the road of seeking justice of any kind that we are duty bound to keep our own hearts free of hatred and despair.

The Irish LGBT exile, through the distorting screen created by a lifetime of conditioning, from religion to culture and everything else, had taught him, her and they throughout history that they were not 'real' men and women. Yes, Joyce is right about history being a nightmare — but it may be the nightmare from which no one can awaken. People are trapped in history sometimes and history is trapped in them. Yet no individual can be taken to task for what history has done. Despite the fact that 'history controls us' and made us who we are, we are at one and the same time privileged and damned by it.

It is necessary to question everything. Everything. As Declan Henry does in this book. It is really quite impossible to be affirmative about anything which one refuses to question; one is doomed to remain inarticulate about anything which one hasn't by the act of imagination, made one's own. It is as easy, after all, and as meaningless to embrace uncritically the cultural sterility of 'Main Street', as it is to decry it. Both extremes avoid the question of whether or not 'Main Street' is really sterile?

We know life is very difficult, very difficult for anybody, anybody born. When we accept our limitations within ourselves and outside of ourselves, we accept we can do something to change these limitations. We are not going to live forever. So within this time called life we are free to do what we can. In accepting the worst, then we can do our best. It seems to me what gets the author through is some kind of faith in life, which is not easy to achieve. This faith in life is more important than lovers, families or friends, riches and vocation. It is, I believe, the rock foundation of all of these. It starts within one's own heart. A covenant of the heart that daily strives not to be bitter or resentful no matter what happens; no matter what the history of injustice or oppression.

What is needed now, I believe, is a church that is on the road, walking, travelling. Not a church that came to a halt, or is turning in circles. A church that is ready to travel on the road of human history, together with the people sharing their history, joys and sufferings. Not a church that is cast down by the load of twenty centuries, but a church of the present, which not only has a history but makes history. A church that accompanies humankind on the road, ready to ask questions, to learn, to listen, ready to be questioned, to discuss, to search. Not a church that is scared or afraid of what happens in people's history, but a church that sees in every challenge a new possibility for creative service.

A church that takes time to be with the people, in which people may exchange their views and experiences, in which uncertainties may be voiced. A church in which people may feel at home, because they feel it is 'their own thing'. A church where questions may remain unanswered, a church that does not dodge the issues, that does not impose the answers. A church strengthened by faith in its Lord. 'Why are you afraid, you people of little faith?' –'Why are you so slow in believing?' A church whose love for God and the people are greater than its fear and little faith. A church that travels even 'until the night falls', that accompanies people even when it gets dark. Not a church that takes its leave when people and things become obscure, but stays with them and shares a meal, shares the people's simplicity and poverty.

Before the sharing of the Bread comes the sharing of life, a sharing of time, of patience, of knowing and searching. Then will people — just as the disciples of Emmaus — get up and go out into the world with renewed joy, strength and hope. Notwithstanding the night, they will take up their responsibility and they will go to their sisters and brothers — wherever they may be — so that in their turn, they can travel with them on the road toward understanding their faith.

Go to the people. Live with them. Learn from them. Love them. Start with what you know. Build with what they have. This is the penultimate message I derived from this most enjoyable book.

FORBIDDEN FRUIT

It started with Adam and Eve in the Garden of Eden after they had forbidden sex. Ever since then the world has quibbled about sex but none more so than the Irish Catholic Church. Up until thirty or forty years ago, almost any type of sex was frowned upon and forbidden. Even if you were married, certain restrictions around contraception were in place.

Fantasies and desires, erections and arousals were swiftly swathed; deemed forbidden and seen as dirty and shameful. Anyone exercising lustful thoughts was considered in need of remorse, guilt and penance to avoid eternal damnation. Frustrated priests, forbidden even to masturbate, preached to people about the morality of sex.

The fruit that grew in isolation from all others was found in the LGBT community — a group of unrecognised beings who lived in a world that greeted them with little welcome.

The malady of clergy paedophilia existed long before it was given a name and long before it came to public prominence. Priests left the fruitless orchard they inhabited and trespassed into illegal lands which were forbidden to enter for good reason.

And then the revolution came and with it brought sweeping change. It started before the clerical sex scandals, although this hastened its speed. The first biggest frontier came crashing down when sex stopped being considered a sin in Ireland. Sex outside of marriage became normal behaviour. The disgrace of unmarried motherhood lost its stigma. Decriminalisation resulted in the LGBT community becoming fully visible. Freedom entered every fibre of society. The reversal of power was exchanged between the church and its people. Secularism, greater wealth and better educated people who were not afraid to challenge hypocrisy in the church saw masses of people turning their back on the church because its fruit had suddenly turned sour.

A few apple trees remain in the orchard but most are withering in the autumn shade. Those still bearing fruit now place less emphasis on sex and sin and mainly refrain from mentioning it, although in the eyes of the church any sex outside marriage is still a sin. But nobody cares anymore. Conflict prevails over the large number of gay priests who are fearful of divulging their sexuality along with the church's abhorrence towards the gay community. The profound loneliness and desperation of priests who are unable to self-regulate their attachment to adolescents and children remains a threat irrespective of the walls that have been erected to prevent trespassing.

Ireland, which was once one of the most Catholic countries in the world, has changed irredeemably. Ireland, where everybody was once under the control of the church, is now free. Only time will tell if there will be a cost for this. For now, it is time to redesign the orchard and plant new fruit that will wholesomely feed the majority and not the minority.

Ireland Today

*For what shall it profit a man, if he gain the whole
world, and suffer the loss of his soul?*
(Jesus)
Mark 8:36

I sometimes wonder if I'm Irish anymore when I compare Ireland
now to how I remember it from my adolescence and early
adulthood. I have now lived outside Ireland for longer than I lived
in it, so my view of the country is more that of an outsider looking
in. However, despite my emigration I have always been a frequent
visitor. So how do I recount the changes that have occurred without
sounding like an immigrant of the past who returned home after
time away, and was shocked to discover everything was different?
I'm not shocked — rather more delighted than saddened by some
of the radical changes that have taken place. The Ireland I left
behind in the 1980s was still steeped in Catholicism and economic
recession. It was far more conservative than liberal. It was a country
that needed new life and change and when these came, they came
in abundance.

The church too has seen many changes — or rather change
has been pressed upon it as a result of no longer having its tight
hold over people. Some believe the damage caused by the clerical
sex abuse scandals and other reputational harm, stemming from
people being suppressed in a pray and obey culture, will never be
undone. In fact, the apathy towards religion in Ireland is at boiling
point. Cricket has never been a sport favoured by Irish people but
now it would be accurate to say there is more interest in cricket
than religion among the general population. The church it seems
has failed to understand how irrelevant religion has become. The
viewpoints and expressions of some people I spoke to bordered on
passive anger. I was told it was time the church was gone because

the clergy are out of touch with the modern world. Others were convinced the Irish Church never listens. This view was shared by some of the priests I interviewed for this book. I will later explore why people turned against their religion, and in the words of W. B. Yeats how 'a terrible beauty was born' that took its place instead.

Yeats was surprised that the deaths of the 1916 revolutionaries led to a reinvigoration of the Irish Republican movement rather than it being dispensed with altogether. Perhaps he would be equally surprised by what happened to the Catholic Church during the last thirty years, which too has been a revolution. There is no camouflaging the fact that Catholicism in Ireland has taken a heavy beating in the past three decades, but in order to understand this you must also consider the societal changes that impacted its dwindling state, irrespective of whether you agree with all, a few, or just some of the changes that have taken place. Some people hope this leads to a reinvigoration of Catholicism in Ireland rather than the religion shrinking any further.

In the past twenty years, Ireland has seen a shift in identity from nationalism to federalism, in that it has fully embraced its role in the European Union. Hence, it has seen the adoption of the euro currency on entry to the European Monetary Union, in contrast to the UK. There was the adoption of the metric system of measurements, e.g. kilometres and hectares replacing miles and acres. There was also the adoption of the European tax year model (which runs from 1st January to 31st December) as opposed to the fiscal year (which runs from 6th April to the 5th the following year).

Ireland has had two female presidents: Mary Robinson and Mary McAleese, who were both liberal, and laid much of the groundwork for social advancement and helped to modernise the country. There have been seismic changes in public attitudes to social issues including contraception, divorce and same-sex marriage. Ireland now has a media which questions far more, without fear, favour or reservation. Social media and the internet has changed everything, making it harder to hide anything. There is terrific choice these days with well-travelled people bringing back new ideas and making the country more open to new cultures and foods.

The abortion referendum in Ireland in 2018 garnered widespread debate but also led to animosity and divided opinion. The Taoiseach, Leo Varadkar, referred to the seismic social and political changes in Ireland as a 'quiet revolution' after 67 percent of the population voted in favour of abortion and 33 percent against. The result indicated a shift has taken place, from the core values historically promoted by the Catholic Church and the Irish state.

In respect of the church, there has been a huge swing away from organised religion, primarily due to the significant amount of clerical abuse cases. Whereas in regard to the state, there has been a swing from right to left, which has produced liberalisation in areas of divorce, same-sex sexuality and the lifting of the medieval blasphemy ban from the constitution.

Many people voted in the abortion referendum for women of the past, for those who hadn't the choice. The vote was based less on religion and more on moral ethos. Young people gave very powerful support to the campaign as women were seen as having control of their bodies for the first time in Irish history. Arguments against the amendment cited less stigma for the unmarried in society, and young males who felt they had lost the right to be fathers if their partners or girlfriends chose abortions. Many people were genuinely shocked and saddened that abortion was legalised. Others were outright enraged, including extreme right-wing groups who targeted GP surgeries that referred patients for terminations and had not opted out of the conscience clause. Demonstrations were organised and rows of white crosses were placed outside surgeries. However, abortion being legalised wasn't totally unexpected given it had been legal in Britain for over half a century, with one in three British females having had an abortion. Additionally, over sixty percent of British Catholics are not opposed to it. In other words, the writing was already on the wall.

I read a newspaper clip recently about assisted suicide which referred to Britain as being backward by not allowing terminally ill people the right to die in their own country, unlike other modern, compassionate countries. Although it didn't name the countries, Switzerland and the Netherlands were the first to drop into my awareness. It also made me think of Ireland and how assisted suicide will be viewed in post-Catholic Ireland in the future. I appreciate it's a sensitive issue, just like abortion is for a great many people. Some will say assisted suicide is a person's individual choice as it is the last bit of dignity they have left. Others may challenge this by saying that nobody except God owns a person's life and that only He has the right to take life. But with all the changes Ireland has seen in the past three decades, could anybody say that assisted suicide will not be passed in a country that has become fearless with change?

▼ ▼ ▼

The future in Ireland will see less children going to Catholic schools. New legislation introduced in 2018 changed the admission criteria, with parents no longer needing a baptism certificate for their child to enter a Catholic primary school from September, 2019. This will mean that schools will no longer be able to use religion as a criterion for prioritising entry. As a result the Catholic ethos in schools is changing with the increased usage of Educate Together Schools (non-denominational) being favoured by parents. While there are currently more of these types of schools in cities, more are expected to roll out nationwide in the years to come. The clergy are not necessarily against this idea. Some are in full agreement because they feel that parents who genuinely want their children to be Catholic will send their child to a Catholic school. New practices are being introduced in modern-thinking schools, including meditation, counselling and spiritual guidance. Non-denominational schools are the way forward with their Religious Education lessons covering all religions. Islam, which is the third largest religion in Ireland, has several state-funded Muslim National Schools in Dublin now, where Arabic, the Qur'an and Islam are taught alongside the national curriculum.

Staying at school until eighteen does not suit everybody but the last twenty years has seen a massive decline in vocational training and apprenticeships in Ireland. However, a renaissance is occurring towards apprenticeships and an earn-and-learn pathway to a skilled qualification. The Junior Certificate is now teacher marked and is considered valueless. University is not academically suitable to every Leaving Certificate student, although many young people are still going to university. It is thought that if you don't have a degree, you are worth less than somebody with one. Even with a degree, job hunting is difficult although internships are more frequent these days as it helps employers to lessen salaries. Inequality is evident among the sexes, with males still being more likely to be selected for top positions and young women with children often being prevented from reaching managerial positions.

Ireland wasn't always considered modern or progressive. In some ways it resembled a developing country up until the 1980s. No jobs, no prospects and limited social welfare meant life for many was a case of barely surviving, resulting in little option but to emigrate for better opportunities and an improved life. Ireland was considered an agricultural country but during the eighties it started to become less common for older sons to succeed their fathers on the farm. Farming up until then was the main source of income for many rural families, particularly for those in the West of Ireland who often laboured hard to make a living. But times changed and paid employment became, for many, a much preferable life than working the land. Farming is still part of the Irish fabric although this too has had its challenges over the years. Bad weather, long hours and poor profits have taken their toll on many small farms. Larger farmers have shifted from dairy to beef farming with emphasis placed on raising higher quality breeds of animals. Even so, many of these farmers still rely on paid employment outside of their farms to make a decent living.

In 1969, Northern Ireland erupted in politically charged violence: over the next 29 years, 3,532 people were killed and 47,541 were injured. People are still scarred by memories of having lived through this brutal conflict. The Good Friday Agreement in 1998 brought ceasefire, resulting in peace for the first time in over 20 years. This had a big impact on Northern Ireland and bordering counties. Life changed dramatically for people in the border counties who gained the freedom to travel without checkpoints. Liberation took place once the cloud of darkness finally lifted. Those born just before or immediately after the agreement was signed became known as 'ceasefire babies', indicative of their generation. The agreement was phenomenal and resulted in a host of small changes that made life simpler and more trusting. There was a complete shift in atmosphere from fear to love. People who were afraid to travel to the North were suddenly able to travel freely. Smuggling of cheaper fuel ended between the bordering counties. People no longer had to have their bags searched (for bombs) every time they entered shops or their cars searched by the Police and the Army every time they crossed the border.

The freedom to travel unrestricted between the Republic and Northern Ireland brought advantages to both economic states. In addition to the tourism benefits, an injection of money from cross-border funding was opened to businesses. Competitive pricing from both sides led to more consumer choice. Over time, both sides of the border became multi-cultural and multi-religious — a big change from the Catholic and Protestant rift which was the sole divide of the past. More non-nationals living in the country resulted in social clubs and adult education centres merging together, lessening cultural divides and creating diversity and integration. The upgrading of roads took place. Cross-border grants were made available from the EU, which led to further structure and economic growth and prosperity. However, the many years of conflict left many scars and there remains a need for conflict resolution and therapy for the traumas endured during the time of the Troubles.

During the 1970s and '80s, much emphasis was placed on having a united Ireland which would comprise of the entire thirty-two counties being under Irish government rule. This was espoused by Sinn Fein, the political party of the IRA (Irish Republican Army). Sinn Fein is the third largest political party in the Republic after the two main parties Fianna Fáil and Fine Gael. Sinn Féin is the second largest party in Northern Ireland after the Democratic Unionist Party (DUP). For many people, a united Ireland is still idealistic rather than realistic because it is felt that both the Republic and Northern Ireland would be financially worse off if this ever occurred. However, that does not preclude Sinn Fein from pressing ahead with this goal, which they say is a legitimate and sensible political objective. Having seen referendums for Scottish Independence and more recently Brexit, Sinn Fein has called on the Irish government to appoint a minister specifically tasked with preparing for a united Ireland. Some of its members are even claiming that Ireland will be united within a generation.

▼▼▼

Prosperity began to descend upon Ireland from the mid-nineties, and the boom years that followed became known as the 'Celtic Tiger'. Banks allowed people to borrow large sums of money without collateral, which made it very easy to acquire property. Some people went from not owning any property to owning several. For many, a second home was an investment. They had no concern about the repayments; particularly the younger generation who had not seen what life was like in the 1980s. People began to be judged on the amount of property they owned and this determined their value and worth. Ireland was in the grips of materialism, greed and ownership. The construction industry scaled great heights and continued to build more and more houses. Every small town in Ireland saw a radical increase in the number of housing estates being built. Jobs were in abundance and high salaries became the norm for building labourers. The country was saturated with money. Nobody had to save for anything as everything was instantly available through borrowing via bank loans and credit cards, resulting in lavish weddings, owning racehorses and Rolex watches becoming a way of life.

The recession had to happen because life in Ireland had spiralled out of control. The Celtic Tiger reached breaking point. There is no doubt many people became rich during the boom years, including politicians, but for many other people the 'crash' meant either personal ruin or immediate, intense financial hardship. Repossessions and bankruptcies became frequent occurrences. Austerity took firm root and became oblivious to misfortune. Banks were bailed out by the government after their money pots dried up. The government then appointed the National Asset Management

Agency (NAMA) to seek a return on the assets and bad debts it inherited from its bailout of the banks.

Housing estates became deserted or derelict. The economy was pushed to tipping point, with fewer jobs for well-educated young people resulting in a swift return to emigration. Ireland had well and truly done a 360 degree turn from being one of the poorest countries in Europe to one of the richest in the world during the Celtic Tiger years, and back again. Now the country had to get used to not being affluent anymore but with the realisation of knowing what it once felt like to be rich. In the meantime, the country was left with a 200 billion euro debt.

Since the Celtic Tiger years, it has been noticed that Irish attitudes have changed, with a lack of civility creeping into daily life. There appears to be a hardening of the heart with widespread compensation claims being made for the slightest issues, and a lack of care and respect for others, particularly the elderly. Crime is on the increase and burglaries upon the elderly have reached a peak. Violence, stabbings and shootings frequently happen in Dublin, Limerick and other large cities.

Homelessness is a big problem in Dublin and other cities, and is at a much higher rate than twenty or thirty years ago. Jesus once said, 'the poor will always be with you' and this is readily seen in the continuous need in Ireland for day centres. Homeless people and families who live in hostels and shelters must vacate them during daytime but have nowhere to go and nothing to do until they can return in the evening. Yet, I have continuously been told that some of these people are the kindest and nicest people, and who have not let disadvantage quench their humanity. Although they experience great suffering, they have great spirit, and despite their displaced lives join with their peers in a sense of community.

On the one hand there is less poverty in Ireland than there was in the 1990s, but poverty these days is more entrenched and less easy to escape from. Up until 30 years ago there were fewer than 1,000 homeless people in Ireland and these mainly consisted of men fallen victim to alcoholism who returned home from England but had lost touch with their families. The landscape of homelessness, alcohol and substance misuse, and general social exclusion has changed drastically since the turn of the twenty-first century. There is now far less unskilled employment than in the past. Consistent poverty exists where individuals are unable to afford meat for their dinner or afford two pairs of shoes or a heavy winter overcoat. It is estimated that 10 percent of Irish children go to school hungry. Hardship is also found in lone parents who are trapped in poverty owing to their inability to work and afford the high cost of childcare. Then there are nearly 2,000 families consisting of 3,500 children who are homeless but are placed in the ever-shrinking rented sector. There is a massive shortage of social housing in what is a dysfunctional housing system. In 1975, the government built 8,500 council houses in Ireland but by 2015 this number had drastically fallen to a mere 75, although a small amount of common sense prevailed in 2018 which resulted in 2,000 being built. But this is not enough to stem the problem bearing in mind the current estimate that there are 186,000 houses boarded up in town and cities throughout Ireland. The private rented sector is unable to cope with the shortage especially as there are fewer properties each year. Those campaigning for homeless people have urged the government to think seriously about housing people who are currently homeless and devise prevention strategies to support those at risk of homelessness. They have also requested that legislation be passed to make it illegal to evict somebody into homelessness. Then there is the problem of the 40,000 homeowners who are in excess of 2 years' mortgage arrears with the Central Bank. It is estimated that at least half of these will eventually result in repossession. There are few Housing Associations in Ireland and a reluctance to introduce mortgage to rent schemes for those at risk of losing their homes.

The government, it is also noted, is in denial of those excluded from society and those who live in poverty, and have made insensitive remarks saying that anybody who has fallen on hard times is the result of years and years of bad behaviour and it is, therefore, their own fault. Days of austerity are now over and, according to the International Monetary Fund (IMF), Ireland is the third wealthiest country in the world per capita. According to campaigners, there is no pressure from the public or the church to tackle poverty. Those excluded from society are simply left behind: lone parents and the unskilled, those with no stable accommodation, and families living on social welfare are expected to make ends meet but remain invisible. Does the church and its clergy (many of which come from middle-class backgrounds) not care about the excluded in society? Historically, it has never been the role of the church — which in the past left social issues to the government to sort out while the state was happy for the church to spread the faith. Do middle-class people not know what it's like to struggle? The answer would seem to be 'not really' because they do not like to be challenged out of their comfort zones. There is still much emphasis on money, family honour and inheritance, and far less importance on individuals calling for social justice. At present, social justice would not appear to be a primary component of the Irish population's present narrative. Nobody really cares that some must survive on precarious working arrangements including variable working contracts with limited hours. Nobody really cares that there is less community in parishes. Only committed Christians care about the excluded in Ireland and even those are distracted as the institutional church edges closer and closer to becoming a lay church, although others, including some priests, feel that the end of a clerical church will lead to a more tolerant and caring society.

Suicide, depression and other mental health issues are big problems in Ireland. It is a particular problem in the under thirties. Young men and women regularly commit suicide by hanging or overdose. The suicide rate for men remains one of the highest in Europe. Depression with an utter sense of hopelessness affects young people who fall victim to this plight. Feeling despondent about the state of the world, combined with having no job and little money, coupled with peer pressure, all adds to poor self-confidence and self-worth. Ireland retains its DNA for being closed and secretive about human suffering. Spending less time with family leaves many with a belief that there is no alternative but death to ease their emotional misery. Priests too have fallen victim, with up to ten priests having committed suicide in the past decade. This would have been unthinkable in the past but the incidence and degree of depression is now much higher than previously. Suicide these days carries less stigma than before and is more openly discussed in society.

The mental health system remains in disarray and often resembles a revolving door that offers no support other than prescribing anti-depressants, even to the very young, despite having adverse side-effects including aggression and suicidal ideation. Illicit drug misuse is also at an epic level. Drugs are a massive problem in every city and town in Ireland. Cannabis is readily available everywhere and anybody wanting heroin or cocaine can get hold of it within ten minutes in the larger cities. In Dublin and other large cities, it is not uncommon to have several generations of a family affected by addiction and mental illness. Some enter the mental health system because of drug addiction and for others addiction is the result of them trying to cope with emotional and mental distress.

People have less time for each other these days. It is felt that there is less listening, caring and compassion in society. The gap between rich and poor is ever increasing. The pension has now been increased to sixty-eight years and is means tested. Medical cards are also means tested and difficult to get if you are unemployed or in low-paid employment. The National Health Service has severe restrictions, and this too is almost means tested. Free hospital treatment is no longer automatic or freely available to every citizen and this sometimes puts enormous financial pressures on people.

▼ ▼ ▼

On the whole, young Irish people have much better self-esteem and think that anything is possible. They also don't feel they have to stay in one place/job for life. There are more women in decision-making positions. The current generation are freer (gay couples can marry) and there are fewer restrictions among families (boyfriends/girlfriends sleeping over is the norm). Young people in Ireland are not afraid to speak their minds and are not people pleasers. They are much more self-assured and positive thinking, and believe that the country has a future. They have less fear of change, allowing for a more flexible approach to managing the economy, government and environmental issues. Their pioneering of technology also sets the country in good stead.

Current times see young people drinking more and having sex younger. Alcohol among young people in Ireland is still a social lubricant and to a degree things haven't changed so much from previous generations in this respect. But these days, young people freely talk about sex and have few inhibitions. Dating apps like Tinder and Bumble are used frequently. Consent workshops take place in colleges and universities. This is in stark contrast to just a few generations ago when sex was denounced as evil and the quickest route to eternal damnation. Society has now well and truly moved on from this type of preaching. Young people now choose freely whether God, religion and church are part of their lives. It's on their terms. The Catholic Church's teachings about sex and sexuality are out of touch with the lives of young people today. Characteristics are also changing in family life. Couples are having fewer children, but it is noticed that children and their parents are better 'friends', and enjoy more openness with each other than their previous generations. However, young people find it difficult to cope with disappointment if they don't get what they want, and haven't got the same resilience as their parents' and grandparents' generations.

Young people are very proactive and with the advantages of social media are not afraid to challenge people or ideals. They challenge officialdom in ways that previous generations were afraid or reluctant to do so. They are good at fundraising and giving. They have a great sense of social justice; they do not want to see somebody fail in life through no fault of their own (illness or accident). They have proved willing and able to raise money for the homeless. The amount of young people leaving Ireland is lessening compared to 10 years ago when dozens left their communities on a weekly basis. Some are now returning and mainly finding in work in Irish cities. There appears to be more work in Dublin. However, on the other hand, businesses are closing with outsourcing to China and India on the increase, but overall the economy is now advancing towards a full recovery. People who emigrate and return seem to appreciate Ireland more than when they left. The unemployment rate that hit over 16 percent after the international bailout, has dropped to 5 percent with good prospects of GDP growth emerging in the coming years.

▼ ▼ ▼

The country has embraced multiculturalism owing to the significant levels of immigration from Eastern Europe and Africa. One in five may now be non-nationals, a tripling in a decade. There are more Polish people now in Ireland than migrants from the UK. Of course, there are those who discriminate against immigrants and who feel the country won't be able to support them. Life for many means choosing between a low skilled, low paying job, or the dole. There are nearly 5,000 asylum seekers and refugees now living in the Republic, although the closed-door policy currently in operation causes some to feel guilty about Ireland's immigration laws given the country's historical reliance on its own emigration past.

Ireland has been a leader in terms of progressive social and lifestyle changes. It was one of the first countries in Europe to introduce the smoking ban and to charge for plastic bags to encourage recycling. Ireland is also in the process of becoming one of the first countries in the world to be totally committed to becoming fossil fuel free. There is a growing shift to renewable energy which will include the banning of cutting turf owing to a growing awareness that harvesting peat emits greenhouse gases which worsen climate change.

Ireland is at the forefront of the world in technology, art and science. It has some of the best universities in the world. Sport is still as prevalent as ever with keen interest in rugby, hurling and Gaelic football. Ireland has always had a deep and rich literary history, and this continues to grow with many new authors joining the ranks including Man Booker prize nominees and winners. Music, dancing and poetry are also at the core of Irish society. The food, fashion and tourism industries are also enjoying growth and success. Aran sweaters these days come in many designs and colours. For some reason, Americans love Aran sweaters. Posters of handsome, athletic young men modelling these sweaters are often seen in shops which prompts purchases from overseas visitors, although few Irish people wear this former fashion favourite, popular in 1970s Ireland.

When anybody who has lived away from Ireland returns, naturally they see structural changes in cities and towns — even in the countryside — with new roads, houses and farm buildings. There are changes everywhere, yet the place still holds a familiar appearance and it is still possible to find parts that haven't changed one iota in the past half century or longer. The most noticeable change of all, though, is the attitude among people. People seem freer, less weighed down, less old fashioned. Despite all the rapid changes, it will take several generations to change the psycho-emotional and sexual state of its nation. Ireland is now freer from the influences of the Catholic Church and seeks to educate and embrace rather than condemn and outcast. However, there are still pockets of its past-DNA which sometimes appears in terms of backwardness, secrecy and judgemental attitudes. The suppressive church of the past is almost like the after effects of poisonous Russian nerve agents (Plutonium and Novichok) whereby forensic examiners still find small traces in the environment long after an attack. Ireland may still have to endure a few more generations before society is fully free of the brainwashing of its past. Of course, there are those who remember the past more favourably than it was, or the opposite, those who bemoan it unfairly. But having said that, images of great progress are easier to recognise in everyday life including a strong visibility of the LGBT community.

Gay people who attended the 2018 annual Pride parade in Dublin told me how they were much encouraged by the positive changes they witnessed. Gay people were supported by parents, grandparents and siblings — even some young family members in pushchairs — all holding both the Irish flag and the rainbow flag. The twenty-fifth anniversary of Pride took place in Dublin where the theme 'We are family' was adopted partly because of the church's hostility towards non-conventional families in Ireland. It turned out to be one of the largest parades in its history with 60,000 people attending. Those present said it was a clear sign that the past is dead and that a new Ireland has been born. It also highlighted the need to re-evaluate how family composition in Ireland is viewed. The church is stuck with viewing family in the traditional sense, as seen at the World Meeting of Families (WMOF) which primarily focused on traditional nuclear families. It is estimated that currently in Ireland twenty-five percent of families consist of same-sex couples with children, lone parent families, and divorced couples who have remarried but share in parenting and families with step-children.

There are some who say that since the Celtic Tiger years, Ireland has become more driven by money than truth-telling as it grew more liberal, wealthier and less religious. Who knows what the future holds? Nobody can forecast how Brexit will impact on Ireland, given the strong trade links with the UK. Ireland is the UK's most significant trading partner for both imports and exports. The UK accounts for €1 billion of Irish trade each week and 1 in 10 jobs. Around 55 percent of Irish exports of timber and construction materials are sold in Britain, along with 50 percent of beef exports and 45 percent of all food and drink sold abroad. Ireland these days is not as heavily reliant on funding from the European Union than in the past. It also has its share of supporters who would vote for withdrawal from the European Union if there was a referendum. It is unlikely, though, that Irexit will come about anytime soon despite Ireland being accustomed to rapid change. The Irish are good at public debating and prior to any referendum that has taken place, ample media and television coverage has been provided in order to help people make an informed choice. Ireland has witnessed the debacle that has beset the UK in negotiating an agreeable withdrawal from the European Union. The people of Northern Ireland voted against Brexit with the majority also sharing this stance in the Republic which values its place within Europe given the financial benefits it has brought the country. The Republic, as well as Northern Ireland, has much welcomed the peace after the Good Friday Agreement, with the idea of going back to hard borders and security checks a dismal thought. During the 1980s, black snow falling from the sky seemed more likely than peace ever occurring in Northern Ireland. Yet peace came and these days people have grown accustomed to it and only a small minority who are drawn towards violence would like to see that jeopardised. But what was also inconceivable was that one day Ireland would arrive at the point where a large number of people would be embarrassed by Catholicism and turn their backs on their ancestral religion.

Having Faith

*Give to everyone who begs from you; and of him who
takes away your goods do not ask them again. And as
you wish that men would do to you, do so to them.*
(Jesus)
Luke 6:30

Particularly in our younger years, a multitude of different life experiences shape our character, as well as influences from parents, friends and teachers. I belong to Generation X — those born during or born between the early-to-mid '60s and early '80s. My generation was often associated with cynicism and rock music and were dubbed the 'MTV' generation. The Sex Pistols and Pink Floyd were the first to cause a change to the music scene in Ireland. Those who started secondary school in the mid-to-late '70s, at a time when corporal punishment was still allowed, will remember the liberating lyrics of 'Another Brick in the Wall' by Pink Floyd: *We don't need no education, We don't need no thought control, No dark sarcasm in the classroom, Teachers leave them kids alone, Hey, teachers, leave them kids alone.* The fear and sight of physical violence from teachers travelled with me throughout my compulsory education in Ireland.

Teachers often misused their power and the profession contained its share of psychopaths who seemingly liked inflicting pain on young people, but this too began to get challenged and discussed in wider society. Corporal punishment was banned in Irish schools in 1982 and in 1996 it became a criminal offence to hit schoolchildren. Many consider the '70s and '80s in Ireland to be a dismal and miserable era. My generation saw continuous economic recession, strikes, unemployment, political upheaval and enduring violence in Northern Ireland. Daily life was often seen as mundane, although sometimes change is not always visible. In hindsight, change was beginning to creep in slowly through literature, music, films, drama and art, bringing gradual acceptance from the wave of secularism coming from the UK, Europe and America. However, there was an acceptance that life in Ireland after secondary school held few opportunities for many young people and therefore emigration continued, although at a lesser pace than in previous generations.

After completing my Leaving Certificate in 1981, that summer was my last one living at home before I left to go to college. Up until that point, I had attended Mass almost every Sunday of my life except for the occasional time I missed because of illness. Attending Mass every Sunday was an integral part of family life in the rural community where I grew up and was an experience shared by everyone I knew. I played my part in our local church from being an altar boy for several years before becoming a lay reader into young adulthood.

My family weren't overly religious. My parents and three older brothers all went to Mass but as a family we weren't the type, unlike many others, who perhaps said the rosary at home. We didn't sign up to the idea shared by others during this era of 'the family that prays together stays together'. However, regular trips to the shrine of Knock loomed at least annually, and this was also the norm growing up and part of the Catholic tradition. This was a special place of worship for Irish Catholics and for visitors from all over the world who came to see the place where The Blessed Virgin Mary appeared in 1879 along with St Joseph and St John the Evangelist. Trips there meant our house had accumulated plenty of religious pictures, statues and crucifixes, although toy cameras and sticks of rock interested me more as a young child. Other religious artefacts were purchased from the missionary priests who visited our parish every year or so and the memorabilia was displayed randomly in each room of our house.

Going to regular confession was also something instructed into us from an early age. The feared words 'Bless me Father for I have sinned' followed by the length of time since the last confessional was rote and mainly meaningless. I hated going to confession and nearly always lied to the priest. It always meant having to make silly things up like who I had lied to or who I stole such and such a thing from before I was released from the confessional box to say perhaps five 'Our Fathers' and five 'Hail Marys' as my penance. It sounds boring because it was boring, but no further thought was put into it until the next confession time was due.

Nobody from my neighbourhood, of my generation, joined the priesthood. Nobody I went to secondary school with joined either. I never had any desire to join the priesthood despite going through the throes of being altar boy and lay reader. It never appealed. However, as a young child I often play-acted at home on Sundays after Mass, pretending to be a priest saying Mass with the ironing board as my makeshift altar. After becoming bored of that, I switched to watching *University Challenge* on our black and white television set with its fixed aerial making it possible to pick up a grainy BBC picture. As I watched bright students answer questions posed by quizmaster Bamber Gascoigne, a desire and imagination grew in me of one day going to university and becoming as clever as those on the programme. It was an ambitious dream given that I never knew any of the answers to the questions. This too phased out when something else caught hold of my imagination. But one thing I always wondered about — how did God call people to the priesthood? I wondered if some big flashing light or some direct words from God beckoned them to join, making them feel adamant they were being called to serve. This wasn't unlike when I was younger when, during Mass, I believed the priest turned wine into blood during the consecration. For many years, I believed that once the consecration was complete the contents of the chalice contained Jesus' blood and that the priest drank his blood at communion time.

But imagination and innocence played only a small part of my early journey in Catholicism. Tales of bizarre rituals and cruelty also held their place. Tales of the churching of women after childbirth was one of these stories. My mother and all other females in my ancestral lineage were made subject to this ritual. Married women (single mothers were exempt) were churched four to six weeks after giving birth, whereby they were made to go to church to receive a blessing by the priest who made the sign of the cross on their foreheads with holy water. Churching derived from a Jewish purification rite, where it was believed that the sin of childbirth was washed away. Many people considered that childbirth made a woman unholy or unclean because it resulted from sexual activity. This practice ended in the late sixties after a raft of changes came into practice resulting from the second Vatican Council.

Up until a few decades before change occurred, mothers often encouraged their sons to become priests. Those sons who succeeded became recipients of a very special reward — the chance of eternal life. On ordination day, the bishop would anoint the hands of the priest with chrism oil before wrapping a purificatory cloth (called a manutergium) around them. This cloth would then be given to the mother and upon her death this would be placed around her hands. Various stories were told about the significance of a mother being given the manutergium after her son's ordination. It was said that once St Peter saw a woman with this hand binding, he would automatically know it was the mother of a priest thus allowing her entrance to heaven without question. According to another tradition, when the mother came before Our Lord, he would say to her: "I have given you life. What have you given to me?" She would hand him the *manutergium* before responding, "I have given you my son as a priest." At this, Jesus would grant her entry into heaven. Fathers, alas, were not included in this privilege and were therefore given nothing.

▼ ▼ ▼

As mentioned previously, suicide remains a big problem in Ireland to the current day, but during the 1970s and 80s, suicide in Ireland, including in my neighbourhood, saw several young men commit suicide by hanging. There was a certain stigma attached to this, although attitudes were changing. For the last few decades, the church had changed its stance on burying suicide victims in unconsecrated ground. But stories were still told of the days when they would have been buried in unconsecrated ground, when the church steadfastly did not want to bury those who committed suicide with everybody else, fearful their sin would contaminate the ground for those already buried in it. Unmarried mothers and/or their babies who died during infancy were buried in unconsecrated ground, and sometimes too, mothers who had not been churched after their baby's birth. Ignorance and cruelty went hand-in-hand in these matters.

It is said that the mystery lived out in Catholicism brings you to the heart of Jesus and the heart of God. There is *no* single unifying structure attached to Catholicism. You can practise it without ever having read the Bible and therefore a person just enters the mystery of it. Catholics hold the saints and the Virgin Mary in high esteem, as well as believing in heaven, hell and purgatory. Catholics believe that the bread and wine of communion become the flesh and blood of Christ through a mystical process called 'transubstantiation'. St Patrick, the patron saint of Ireland, firmly believed in the Trinity of the Father, Son and Holy Spirit being considered part of the one Godhead. St Patrick compared the Trinity to the shamrock because the plant had one stem and three leaves. Reverence to saints in Ireland was an extra chore when maintaining one's faith, whether it was devotion, for example, to St Anthony, St Francis, St Aloysius or Padre Pio. While everybody celebrated St Patrick's Day, St Patrick himself seldom seemed to receive the same level of devotion given to other saints in terms of novenas and relics. With all these pious figures to pray to for intercession to God, Catholicism could seem a little overcrowded at times. Although harmless, it equated to wearing an extra layer of clothing when it wasn't warranted by the weather. But it seemed this was a fear people had developed about God that an intermediary was sought to negotiate and deliver prayers on their behalf. Although I liked stories about saints and their lives, I realised at some point that putting them on par with the upper echelons of deity didn't make sense. Cutting out this middle piece, I streamlined my belief system to God, Jesus and Our Lady, avoiding the roundabout way via the saint route.

In Ireland of yesteryear, there only seemed to be two strands of Christianity. A person was either Catholic or Protestant. A few broke ranks and joined new age born-again Christian cults that occasionally popped up, which were loathed with a vengeance by the Catholic clergy. But hatred of any cult could never be matched with that held for Protestants. It seems nonsensical that disdain remained in our ancestral lineage when both faiths held so many similarities. Growing up in the 1970s and '80s meant enduring a daily round of media reporting of bombs and killings in Northern Ireland by the IRA and other paramilitary terror groups. The brutality was endless to the point that people living in the Republic became anaesthetised towards this civil war, partly because we were separated from its daily horrors and partly because most weren't preoccupied with the country becoming a united Ireland. Northern Ireland, because of its troubled history, had become the prodigal relative that didn't fit in with the peaceful safety enjoyed by the Republic.

▼ ▼ ▼

After I left home and started working in the catering industry, I only occasionally attended Mass because my working hours clashed with the times Mass was being said. But gradually over a year or so, my attendance dwindled to the point that, without realising it, I had stopped going altogether. I had unintentionally joined the secular world. My attendance since then has been totally sporadic but has mainly consisted of attending Mass a few times a year. I am what you call a lapsed Catholic or more accurately a non-practising Catholic. But at no point have I stopped being spiritual, nor have I stopped looking for answers to life and the divine. I remember first coming to London in the mid-eighties and being at Speakers' Corner in Marble Arch with an Irish friend. A man was reading from the Bible and before giving us a leaflet with a prayer on it, he asked if we would say the prayer with him. I was fine with this, but my friend refused and began to walk away before I followed, but not without feeling annoyed at his stubborn behaviour. This made me realise, however, how open I was to other forms of religion besides Catholicism. Later, when I went to live in Australia for a year, I encountered The Church of Scientology and while this opened my mind to many interesting facts about spirituality and how the mind works, its shortfall for me was its neutrality on God. How do you believe you are a spirit who has lived many previous lifetimes but do not have a creator? It simply didn't make sense to me.

I still have a leaning towards the Catholic Church more than any other Christian denomination. Even now as a non–practicing Catholic, I have never lost my belief in God or Jesus which have remained steadfast throughout my life. Over the years, friends have invited me to Anglican Church services, but when I attended these, I have always felt I was intruding upon a gathering where those present knew I did not belong to their group. Simply, this is because I feel most at home in Catholicism because this is the faith shared by my parents, grandparents and ancestral Irish lineage.

I often wonder what direction my peers from the 1980s have taken in their faith. Based on our age group in relation to church attendance, around 40 percent still attend Mass. But is this through commitment to the church, a sense of obligation or for keeping up appearances, as part of a habit? The other 60 percent will have given up on the church for various reasons, seeing the church as irrelevant, outdated, and not part of their lives. They grew up experiencing the church as an institution focused on lamenting about the past, all the while using 'tired' and 'worn out' forms of language — rather than forms of expression and communication which connected with them. Ultimately, lives have changed so radically in the past thirty years with everything becoming fluid; for example, secularism, clerical sex abuse scandals or disagreement with church teachings which seem out of touch especially on issues like homosexuality, divorce, remarriage and same sex marriages. Many of those who turned their backs on the church will have been victims of clerical abuse or were related to its victims. Most churches are only a third full for Sunday Mass, the main attendees are women, and the age group consists of late to middle-aged and elderly people who remain trapped by the old indoctrination of fear-based teachings; fearful of dying in sin and not going to heaven. Young people have grown up with negative media reporting about paedophile priests and the horrors of clerical child abuse, resulting in them turning away from the institutional church. These days, few teenagers attend Mass, and attendance numbers further decline once they have made their confirmation.

▼▼▼

In a historical context, Ireland should be viewed as a land that lost its soul since the time of the famine. It lost its language, and people were often made to feel like outsiders living in their own country. Treated by the British as being inferior, the country had developed a third world type of mentality. When independence from Britain finally arrived in 1922, people cherished a new sense of freedom, as much as independence. But it still wasn't free. The Catholic Church remained in place like a stern parent ever ready to discipline its child, even when it didn't need disciplining. Priests held power and status up until the 1990s.

My generation was the last one to have grown up under the old regime which meant nobody ever criticised or challenged the Catholic Church either through respect or fear. For many centuries in Ireland there was no separation between the church and its people. The church censored everything including books, films and television programmes. Neither was there any separation between church and state. The church exerted control over many things, including the education system. This resulted in the Irish being a population with a low level of awareness about sex, homosexuality and many other aspects of life in general.

▼▼▼

Later in this book, I discuss clerical sex abuse but it is also important to highlight the sobering thought that 88 percent of all child abuse, whether it is physical, emotional or sexual, is committed in families. The biggest number of sex abusers being fathers, brothers and uncles. One out of every four people in Ireland have been affected by abuse but these days it is recognised in society, spoken about, action is often taken and perpetrators brought to justice. In the past none of this occurred. However today, Ireland is a far freer nation after the experience of years of unmitigated misery, suffering and oppression. The secrets of the past were truly appalling and while some of these were unearthed, others may remain hidden forever. Ireland is historically a violent society. Abuse and violence are not unrelated, and, in the past, it was not considered sinful to beat a child. Victims suffered in silence. It was tolerated and justified. It might be difficult to now imagine that the Ireland of the past was a violent and supercilious macho culture. Irish masculinity did not permit any sort of touch if intended in a gentle, friendly or loving way. This was left to mothers and they too sometimes struggled. Irish men had a real problem with feelings and an inability to express them. Physical contact was confined to sports and fights. Some men experienced terrible violence through heavy beatings. It was mainly through violence that men could touch, although sometimes this had a sadistic side to it. Often loneliness, depression, emptiness and desperation were commonplace. Sexual repression and frustration meant bestiality was also an unspoken reality in rural areas. The stigma of mental health was ever present but hidden and silenced along with its many signs and symptoms. The complete ban on contraception up until the 1960s and early '70s meant it was not uncommon for couples to have extremely large families which often led to severe financial suffering and hardship, as well as other serious problems.

▼ ▼ ▼

Catholics of the past were expected by the clergy to adhere to a type of theology that kept them in the dark. They weren't allowed to question or challenge anything. In fact, the thought of either would never have occurred to them having been brought up in a climate of deep respect for the church. Nobody was encouraged to become acquainted with theology or read the Bible. Instead, the church focused on rules, control and instilling a sense of fear, with many priests preaching that the gates of hell were waiting for those who committed such and such a sin, mainly sex-related sins. People who were knowledgeable in many subjects remained ignorant about theology, with many reaching adulthood and still retaining a child's view of it.

The Catholic Church through its hierarchical and controlling features developed a strain of 'Jansenism' in its theological stance. This was adapted from a movement in France who favoured the stricter teachings of St Augustine (often recognised as a cantankerous theologian), who placed heavy emphasis on sin, human depravity, the necessity of divine grace and heaven and hell. Priests rarely spoke of God's love and compassion. The effects of this on Ireland meant it became a land of confessions, continuously deciphering what was venial sin and mortal sin. It became obsessed with immorality, where even getting an erection was seen to be sinful. The answer to maintaining purity was joining a pious organisation that carried out some charitable kind of work. This was encouraged to blank out impure thoughts of sex while carrying out good work for the benefits of others.

For the greater part of my childhood, the reigning pope was Pope Paul VI up until his death when he was succeeded by John Paul I, who then died shortly after taking office. The next pope, though, was to make his mark in ways different to those of his predecessors. Breaking a long tradition of popes always being Italian, a handsome and charismatic Polish man, Karol Józef Wojtyla, took everybody by surprise. I vividly remember the summer of 1978 when the world became witness to the new head of the Catholic Church — Pope John Paul II. From the outset, he seemed different to what was expected of a pope; he seemed approachable, likeable and human. He had been an actor in his younger life, wrote poetry and had a girlfriend before joining the priesthood. His visit to Ireland the year after taking office heralded widespread support, joy and pride that the pope was coming to visit our country.

Except for Poland (where abortion was used as a form of contraception) no other Catholic country was as backward or oppressed in its religion as Ireland. Pope John Paul II remained a very likable pope throughout his papacy and garnered widespread sympathy during his ailing health in the final years of his life. Like all popes, to the papal throne, he brought character traits born of his own unique life experiences and learnings. He helped defeat communism in Poland and while in office concentrated on liturgical issues like how the sacraments were celebrated. However, despite being canonised a saint by Pope Francis, his legacy has been found to be less than favourable. Cozzens (2000) stated that bishops who worked with John Paul mentioned how he explicitly forbade them to ever discuss contraception, abortion, homosexuality, the lifting of celibacy in the priesthood or the ordination of women unless they were defending the church's official teachings. There simply wasn't a space allowed to openly debate these issues with a view to reform and change.

Even in regard to sex within marriage, the Catholic Church has always had a negative view towards sex. Earlier it was described how up until the 1960s, after giving birth, married women were 'churched'. They realised that procreation was necessary for mankind to continue but childbirth meant having sex. Though a married couple having sex for the purpose of procreation wasn't itself considered sinful, the ever present possibility of sexual enjoyment provided a reason for frowning upon such activity — as well as insinuations being made about it being a sinful behaviour. Equally baffling was the church's teaching on contraception. I grew up listening to them speak about the Billings Method as their preferred choice of contraception. Really, how could celibate priests — who had purportedly never had sex in their lives (and/or were never supposed to in the future) — be sufficiently knowledgeable to advise about such matters? Therefore, the Catholic Church regularly advertised that their preferred contraception method encouraged married women to recognise their own fertility patterns, enabling them to choose when to avoid sex to prevent pregnancy or when to have sex in order to conceive. I have no idea how many women listened to this advice but the arrogance and assumed superiority of the church was wholly inappropriate.

▼▼▼

When Frank McCourt wrote *Angela's Ashes* (his memories of growing up in Ireland — which was published in 1996) he remarked, '*Worse than the ordinary miserable childhood is the miserable Irish childhood and worse yet is the miserable Irish Catholic childhood.*' Here I disagree with McCourt because being heterosexual, he never considered what it would have been like to have grown up gay in Ireland — in the decades before the LGBT community became more acceptable. Let me fill in the missing gap. Being gay was very difficult and often painful. It meant growing up without a day going by when invisibility wasn't the norm. Homosexuality wasn't part of our education system. The possibility of being gay wasn't part of our early socialisation and wasn't part of how we viewed the world. The opposite meant we were expected to think and act like heterosexuals, which was considered the norm. Gay people were simply expected to remain 'invisible'.

I resonate with the words of Fr Bernárd Lynch, who wrote the foreword to this book. Bernárd, an openly gay Irish priest now living in London, recalled the Ireland of the past by saying that up until recent decades, the moment a gay person was born, their heart automatically went into reverse mode owing to the heteronormative environment they were born into. Bernárd added that it is only children born now who will be allowed to grow up with free hearts. As a teenager, my heart was never free. Like so many other gay people of my generation, as a matter of survival, I kept my heart securely guarded and hidden. It wouldn't be an exaggeration to say gay people were modern day lepers in Ireland. Only years later, after being able to step back and reflect on events, have I been able to make better sense of things. When you study the life of Jesus you realise that he too was an outsider. He mixed with tax collectors and prostitutes. Jesus was a real man who closed the gap between God and humanity. Jesus did not cast judgement on others, rather he accepted people as they were. It's a shame the church could never bring itself to preach the same message, despite many priests, which I will discuss later in greater detail, themselves being homosexual.

I had a lovely childhood and loving parents. In some ways, it was idyllic growing up on a farm in the West of Ireland, free from violence and hunger. But it also meant growing up in a country where discussion about homosexuality was enduringly silent. Parents never mentioned it to their children and vice versa. Parents like their children to fit in with society and other peers and my parents were no different. So, in order to seem like everybody else, I wore a mask, and like many others of my generation my sexuality had to remain unexpressed and invisible, meaning outwardly I was one person and inwardly another. I had a heart that contained a secret for as long as I could remember. This resulted in disappointment time and time again for myself and others because there was always a part of me that could never be fully revealed. I'm not describing Ireland here in the nineteenth century, although by today's standards it might sound like that. This was Ireland during the seventies and eighties and indeed the decades that preceded them. It was simply intolerable, fearful and unnecessary.

It was a Sunday evening and not long after I had left home, I began feeling lonely and confused, and in need of a little comfort. I went to the local priest's house in the area that I was living in at the time to see if I could talk to him in the hope that some of my burden would be lifted. I can't recall exactly what I had intended to tell him, but it was highly unlikely that I would have told him I was gay for fear of being rejected and ridiculed. I was just seeking somebody to talk to and perhaps in a roundabout way find comfort. There were no awkward moments in our conversation other than the one that greeted me after I knocked on the door. The priest answered and I asked if I could speak to him. He immediately replied that it wasn't possible because his dinner was cooking and he had to keep an eye on it. His abrupt reply brusquely ended my visit without the priest even asking if I wanted to come back another time. That was the end of me ever seeking solace from any priest. Looking back on this now, I smile at my naivety of going to the priest in the first place, but also wonder if any other gay person ever did the same.

During research for this book, I asked a priest what he would say if a young gay person came to him, struggling with their sexuality and asking for advice on how to cope. There was an awkward silence and clearing of the throat before he eventually replied that he would support them in telling their parents. Basically, he didn't know how to respond to my question despite him having been a school chaplain at one point. This made me think priests may have seldom been approached for guidance or advice in such matters, because of how uncomfortable young people would have felt on approaching them. However nowadays, I suspect that if anybody suggested to a young gay person they speak to a priest about their sexuality, it would be considered incredulous and probably provoke laughter.

Both then and now, priests, especially those who are gay, have been spared seeing their own reflection as a result of not helping others confront and address their sexual orientation. What angers me though, is how the Catholic Church still denounces homosexuality as if it is a problem outside of themselves. You will see in later chapters, this is anything but the case. The damage the church has done, and continues to do to gay people is shocking. This denial and hypocrisy remain absurd — and such denial and hypocrisy is shameful and untenable, to say the least. Did priests preach about homosexuality when I was growing up? In my experience they never directly mentioned the word in sermons. Occasionally, a missionary priest visiting our parish would reflect about the sin of masturbation where inevitably every teenager in the congregation, including myself, would cringe at the embarrassment of this being discussed. What sin? What stupidity in not thinking it normal for teenagers to masturbate. Did he never masturbate himself when he was a teenager? So, the priest spoke nonsense and everybody in the parish turned up and listened. But knowing what I know now about priests, I am assuming they kept away from the subject of homosexuality because it was too close to home for many. Even if a priest wasn't gay themselves, they must have encountered homosexuality at some point in their ministry or would, at the very least, have discussed it in private conversations with other priests.

Clergy

So, I say to you, Ask and it will be given to you;
search, and you will find; knock, and the door
will be opened for you.
(Jesus)
Luke 11:9

The Irish Church, which is a hierarchically structured organisation that is central to Irish identity, is bleeding from a lack of priests. There are hardly any priests in their thirties, very few in their forties, quite a few in their fifties and the majority in their sixties, seventies and eighties. Priests across Europe are depleted in number. The situation in Ireland is no different to France, Germany or Holland. The strong winds of secularism over the past fifty years have seen society breaking loose from religious institutions and organised religion. Therefore, it would be wrong to place the entire blame for decreased church attendance on the clerical sex abuse scandals, rather it seems more likely such events provided some people with an excellent excuse for no longer going to Mass (presuming their faith had already lapsed).

For a great many people, the days are over of being 'a good Catholic', meaning regular church attendance and agreeing with the dogma that divorce and homosexuality are immoral. Such persons generally acted like an automaton which hadn't the capability to discover any spiritual knowledge outside the Catholic Church. And only for a few elderly parishioners, mostly women, is the remaining custom of clutching rosary beads and reciting prayers by rote. This robotic habit which lacks any kind of divinity, is also in its final days because of the plethora of middle-aged people who have already left the church, which leaves little room for more elderly followers to take their place.

Although most priests in Ireland are elderly and conservative, there are also liberal priests of all ages. Liberal priests (and outspoken priests) can be found in the Association of Catholic Priests (ACP), which is a sort of 'trade union' for priests set up in 2007. It is estimated that over a quarter of Irish priests are members. Most are broadminded and some are outspoken in the media on issues regarding ordination of women, lifting of celibacy and homosexuality. Members give moral support to each other and look out for each other in the absence of help from their bishops or the curia. However, the curia dislikes the ACP and has asked priests to forfeit their membership. Bishops have tended to avoid contact with the ACP and none have ever become a member.

Many elderly priests run parishes by themselves. With a constant struggle for diocesan vocations, the future looks grim. Often these mechanically produced priests who were ordained in the sixties and seventies can't cope with changes in the church and in society. Some of them that I spoke to wondered if, after they die, there might be no alternative but to replace them with Nigerian priests. However, though numbers are higher than they used to be, it looks unlikely that a surplus of priests from Africa or Asia will be arriving, owing to visa requirement restrictions to do with the immigration of foreign preachers.

I spoke to priests who felt demoralised by their job. They were embarrassed and felt they had lost credibility. Many readily admitted that what the church says about contraception, gay people and the ordination of women priests is nonsense. This is just part of a general weariness felt by the priests of all ages who remain in the church. They face continuous bombardment by the media resulting in them feeling humiliated and losing confidence in themselves. They feel confronted and battered from every side in the aftermath of the clerical abuse scandals. One priest, Fr Tom, referred to the piece in the Mass which states 'Lift up your Hearts', adding that this is easier said than done and how he could no longer be expected to preach a cheerful little message without addressing the truth.

Amongst others, the clerical sex abuse scandals involving clergy who had fathered children was another factor in the decline of Catholicism in Ireland. It hurt many people, including good priests, but most of all caused long-lasting hurt for the reputation of the church, from which it has never recovered. Several Irish people I interviewed were unable to speak well of priests, stating that they often found them to lack understanding and compassion with some describing them as cantankerous, miserable and sharp. Others, however, recognised that priests are hardworking and that despite the 'downfall' in the reputation of the church there is still a lot of goodwill shown towards priests. Some recognised that bishops have a tough job keeping parishes and dioceses active and running. Others referred to diocesan priests having an ambivalent relationship with their bishops and are not always regarded as the best people to care. For many Irish people, priesthood is about keeping a community together, reaching out to the sick, administering the sacraments (particularly those to children) and encouraging young parents with children to come to church and to offer informal counselling to distressed individuals. But priests too need to unwind and have support structures in their lives, including family, friends, hobbies, as well as interests outside of the church. As you will see later in the book, loneliness, isolation and burnout leads to emotional imbalances.

In comparison to few in the '80s (before the economic turn-around), many Catholic foreign nationals are now living in Ireland, including Polish, Slovakian, Lithuanian and Indian. Arjun, my taxi driver, was from India. After entering his car, I instantly noticed rosary beads wrapped around the driver's mirror. Upon enquiry, he confirmed he was a Catholic and had lived in Ireland for over ten years. He was married with two daughters and was planning a holiday back home to get his baby daughter baptised. His parents, siblings and extended family live there, and a large party was planned for the christening. Catholicism is a minority religion in India but those who practice it are devout. Young men enter seminaries at the age of seventeen when they complete secondary school. A lifetime of celibacy and devotion await them. Parents are proud of their son priests for making this sacrifice. According to Arjun, there is no mention of clerical sex abuse scandals in India. Occasionally there are a few stifled giggles if somebody makes an innuendo about a bishop having a nun as a girlfriend. Now, doesn't this little story remind you of what life was like in Ireland fifty years ago?

In past times the reasons for joining the priesthood included spiritual motives for young males who were pious and felt a calling. It was also seen as a good career choice with status and social standing. It was also a good way to avoid marriage if you were gay or if you wanted to receive a good education (seminarians studied theology, philosophy and canon law to degree level), or for those who wanted to travel on the missions, there were religious orders who recruited. It was automatically, although foolishly, believed that the young men who were usually aged around seventeen or eighteen were straight, yet often young men entering the seminary had no real consciousness about their sexual orientation and had never thought about it. In the past there was a complete failure to screen seminarians. It was taken at face value that those wanting to join the priesthood had heard God's call and therefore they were not questioned any further. The gates of the seminary were opened to the insecure, immature and psychologically disturbed, who in those days entered in their droves. And it was here that their journey towards the priesthood began by living a lonely celibate life in a hierarchical institution surrounded by snobbery and spitefulness and sometimes with no chance of ever making real friends.

Why was it expected that these young men turn out well-adjusted under these circumstances? Instead it often produced repressed and socially awkward individuals who had little knowledge of love or women and as they matured into adulthood became fearful of themselves, fearful of sex and fearful of desires. This appalling lack of education and training in these human and sexual matters left many with a handicap of the heart where they were unable to feel, understand or express love. Yet, these men were destined, because of their training, to be a paragon of the virtues they were preaching. They were regarded as the moral fibre of society whereby there was no moral ground higher than the church, its priests and what they preached.

▼▼▼

Priesthood is often viewed as a lonely life and one that is under-valued. But one thing most Irish priests have in common is they en-

counter a wide-ranging plethora of experiences during their ministry. Some of those I interviewed shared some faith stories with me.
Fr Liam told me the story of a man whose deathbed he attended, so
as to administer the last rites. The man had been baptised Catholic
but had not practised for much of his life and now that he was close
to death had asked to see a priest. Liam came across as a lovely,
laid back and friendly priest. I imagined how lucky the dying man
would have been to have him at his side. Liam told me this story as
an example of how Christ clings to a person so that they enter his
kingdom. This also serves, he said, as an example of how a baptised
Catholic always remains a Catholic and highlighted how this man
who had spent his life apart from the church decided to rejoin it at
the end of his life. Liam also pointed out that priests enter people's
lives at various points, sometimes at the beginning and sometimes
at the end. Liam said that as a priest he felt his role was about embracing God, religion and life — and planting these seeds in those
who he was honoured to meet during his ministry, irrespective of
their needs or circumstances.

Fr Paschal told me a story about Pope John XXIII. The pope was
once giving a papal audience to a congregation of over a thousand
people. Suddenly his attention was drawn towards a priest leaning
against a pillar. He noticed there was something lonely and forlorn
by the way the priest looked. The priest looked out of context to
others around him and this intrigued the pope. The pope asked one
of his officials to go to the priest and requested he came to see him
after the audience had ended. The priest was very flattered by the
pope's request and, after greetings, the pope asked him if there was
something worrying him. The priest replied, "I attended someone
today who was dying. The man is lapsed in his faith and he has
refused the sacraments for the dying." He added, "This has worried
me so much because I fear his soul will be lost forever." The pope
entered in a discussion with the young priest and reminded him
that he was ordained to preach the gospels, minister the sacraments
of the church and to be a shepherd to his flock. In doing so, he
would see many circles unfolding — birth, confirmation, marriage
and death. The pope asked what happened when these gifts were

refused before advising the young priest that all he could do was to carry on with his ministry and entrust people to God's mercy. Even the pope admitted that he didn't know the mystery of the cross after death, telling the young priest that people only ever know what is on this side of it.

Fr Adrian told me that as a priest he constantly sees the love of God poured into people's lives and that as a priest he constantly helps others on their way. His role as a prison chaplain allowed him to meet so many different people of various nationalities and backgrounds. He met many suicidal people in his ministry and often met up with them some time afterwards when they asked him, "remember what you said?", before reiterating some forgotten words of hope he had given them at that low ebb in their lives. Adrian said, every day in the priesthood is different. Each night before he says his prayers he reflects on the day and its events. Adrian concluded that he tries to do his bit to help people find God so they can change their own lives.

But not all callings are the same and no two priests are alike. A person need only consider the different personalities of the twelve apostles to realise this. Some believe the gospel must be preached in whatever context we live, whether this is during wars, uprisings, terrorism and famine. Other priests told me that the priesthood needs to be a cradle of kindness consisting of pastoral care, as well as placing the liturgy into a context which is sensitive to people's lives. They believe that the preaching message must be uplifting. A few priests jokingly told me priests need to be more cheerful, laugh more and enjoy a glass of wine. Some priests believe that going to Mass should be a joyous occasion with music and singing to make Jesus' presence real in the hearts of people. All created existence begins in God and therefore you must create an environment at Mass that has a sense of wonder and awesomeness. The church has lost this ability to express how God's word speaks to the world. When we say the 'Our Father' prayer, we become one mind with Jesus and how he viewed the reality of the world through human eyes. This is a two-way movement — praying the prayer of Jesus and becoming the prayer because you are going back to the mind of Jesus.

Many priests reminded me that in local communities, throughout Ireland, priests remain central to this but (hopefully) not in the hierarchical way of the past. The church must be in touch with the issues of the real world — the here and now. The role of the priest is to work with people and to identify their gifts. Many felt priests should be considered by parishioners as great teachers, dispensing precious pearls of wisdom. Some even seem to conceive of this as God being brought to people, not the other way around. Partnerships formed between the priest and his parishioners is the way faith is grounded together along with the liturgy, being attentive to the poor and the environment because God is obvious in every dimension of life.

Up to a million people in Ireland still go to Mass every week. There are others who no longer regularly go to Mass but attend christenings, weddings and funerals. I have spoken to priests who commented on the decline in Mass goers and said people should remember they won't be judged on how the clergy of the past acted, they will be judged on how they themselves act. One priest, Fr Peter, spoke of his devotion in living out the gospel irrespective of the number who show up for weekly Mass. He said he tries his best to bear witness to Jesus to his parishioners. Peter added that some people find it hard to accept that Jesus came to show us the way, but that this is why during the consecration of the bread and wine at Mass the words are said, "Do this in memory of me". Peter said he feels the person of Jesus as explained in the gospels is missing in people's humanity these days — and that the church needs to take responsibility for the situation.

▼▼▼

When I was young, priests were generally held in great esteem. Nobody dared to call a priest by their first name. My young mind thought they were men who God had called to serve the church. Priests, who were able to turn wine into blood, hear confessions and forgive sins, anoint the dying as well as baptising and marrying people. Only those who were special in God's eyes were called to this duty. They had a vocation. They had received a sign from

God that they were among his chosen ones who were closer to him than ordinary people. I now know how this sounds — a fanciful fairytale — but like so many others I had once believed this to be true. I asked some priests why they had chosen the priesthood.

Fr Michael, now in his fifties, said living in Dublin was a big change from his upbringing in rural Ireland resulting in him turning more to his faith. He was lonely despite having many friends, including a girlfriend. He felt lost and began going to Mass every day either at lunchtime or in the evening. Michael said he was always a bit of a worrier but when he attended Mass he felt peace, support and protection. Gradually he began to feel closer to God. Some friends suggested the priesthood and although in hindsight this was the start of sowing seeds in his mind, at the time he didn't give it much consideration. Life ticked along at work, and at weekends he went home to his parents. Then one day at Mass, he remembered coming out of church and feeling a tremendous peace that he had never felt before. It was just an indescribable feeling — a glimpse of heaven. In fact, it felt like he was transported to heaven and felt the presence of God, so profound was the experience. Michael went to see a priest to talk to him about the priesthood but to his surprise, the priest wasn't the least bit encouraging and kept changing the conversation, and at one point asked him what he would be having for dinner that night. Somebody told Michael later that the priest might have been deliberately off-putting, knowing that if Michael's calling was real, his cavalier attitude wouldn't be a deterrent. The next morning Michael woke feeling troubled and ill at ease. The feeling was stronger than ever. This unrest was followed by a further feeling of peacefulness signalling his need to act. So he made up my mind that he would join the priesthood. Michael feels the greatest gift he offers as a priest is giving Jesus to people during Mass and Holy Communion. And that has remained the case over the past quarter of a century, despite the tumultuous times the church has witnessed. He is still happy being a priest and it has brought him a closer understanding of God. He said that praying, along with having a supportive family and circle of friends, has sustained him during the difficult times and has made him realise how blessed he is in this regard.

Fr Peter, now in his seventies, trained in the 1960s at a time when the Irish clergy were up there (pointing upwards) and the people were down there (pointing downwards). Priests were generally differential. They talked to you as opposed to you talking to them. In those days there were just three well-educated people in the parish — the doctor, the teacher and the priest. He remembered as a young boy serving Mass when mothers would come to the priest asking them to read out loud the letters they had received from their sons in England. Later, he discovered that the sons in England also went to their priests to write the letters which they sent to their mothers. Only three, including Peter, from his class at National School went on to secondary school. Boys who didn't go to secondary school went to work on building sites and the girls became servants. At secondary school he remembered a visiting priest telling his class about all the wonderful jobs they could do after they finished their education, but the best job of all was to become a priest. Soon afterwards Peter started wearing rosary beads around his neck, so proud he was of being Catholic. He said his vocation germinated from that point. Those who completed secondary school often ended up going into the civil service. And then there were those whose lives were marked out to be priests. Peter said he was always poor at Latin and even in those days boys had to learn Latin to become an altar service, let alone a priest. He remembered one of his teachers telling him he feared he would fail Latin which would mean he wouldn't be allowed to join the seminary. Peter eventually managed to scrape a pass. He remembered being heartbroken leaving his parents, brothers and sisters when he first entered the seminary, but he soon got used to the routine and made new friends.

Peter and his fellow seminarians were told upon entering the seminary that a third would leave, a third would be thrown out and a third would make it to the end. In the end, out of a class of sixty — twenty-one of them were ordained. They were instructed not to make any special friends in case anyone left. This was hard at times because in those days they had to share a room with another seminarian. When somebody left, they were never told what had happened, but it always seemed to be the bright ones who suddenly disappeared without any further word. Those who were thrown out were usually those who preferred football, beer and women to theology lessons! Peter said he later realised that a lot of these young men were never suited to be priests. It was their mothers who wanted it to be their vocation. Every year during his seminary years he would go home and spend the three summer months working on his father's farm. He would go to dances and pubs. They were encouraged to socialise — to sample life — to ensure that they knew what they were giving up was right for them. And when they returned each September, the superiors would interrogate Peter and other seminarians about what they did, what they experienced, their thoughts and feelings. They wanted to see how the young men operated in society outside the confines of the seminary walls and if they were able to resist the temptations of life without ever alluding to what exactly they were referring to in their questioning. In hindsight, Peter said it were perfectly clear what they were alluding to — women, sex and marriage. Peter concluded by saying that he has a truly wonderful life — filled with travel and discovery. He said he has met every kind of person imaginable. Priesthood for him has encapsulated meeting people who have experienced every type of human problem. He has seen the darkest hour and has often spent it with people until it passed.

▼ ▼ ▼

History tells us that several of the twelve apostles were married and had children. St Peter, who was often considered the first pope, was married and had a family. After that, several other popes were married with children. The Catholic Church was a thousand years old before celibacy was introduced and gradually began spreading in the Western Church in the Middle Ages. Celibacy was offering something special and considered a true human sacrifice. Although priests could marry before the Middle Ages, not all popes held a positive view about sex and relationships with some earlier popes commenting that all sexual desires were sinful and evil. Once celibacy was made compulsory, desires and fantasies were considered to be the work of Satan and all sexual urges of priests had to be repressed.

However, the main idea behind introducing celibacy was that the church did not want married priests handing over church property to wives and children. Spain was one of the first countries to make this mandatory, with others following suit by making it a prerequisite of the job. Priests were instructed to consider the spiritual dimensions of celibacy, as a balance to the huge sacrifice they were making. As a consolation, they were told that virginity was deemed superior to marriage in the eyes of the church. However, this failed to acknowledge that for most priests joining a seminary, such an undertaking would mean a lifelong journey in which their soul would long for a union and intimacy, which in many cases would remain unfulfilled outside of an intimate relationship.

Fr Frank said that in the past there was a negative understanding of sexuality and although celibacy has for some been valuable, in the main it has had disadvantages. For many the pastoral life has proved an unattractive option, living in a big house while experiencing loneliness. This has led to some priests turning to alcohol for comfort. This fate did not fall upon Frank who said that if he had his life over again he would have liked to have been married. He admitted when he was a younger priest that he hoped the pope would remove celibacy but accepts it has never happened and for him it is now too late. He doesn't feel bitter and has reconciled this is the path he has chosen to remain on and that, in the main, he has lived a happy enough type of life.

Fr Chris said he made the choice to be celibate but admitted that when he was younger physical attractions were there for women. Temptations were sometimes difficult to handle but he succeeded and never once wandered off course. Chris joked that he was at a retreat once, where the facilitator told the priests that the devil always places attractive feet at the feet of priests — but that, personally, he had never had the experience. I asked him if the devil also placed attractive men at their feet too, but the suggestion appalled him. He went on to say, "Priests shouldn't be allowed to marry — because celibacy isn't the problem it is made out to be — as sex isn't everything". He continued, saying that it's a self-sacrifice but priests adjust to celibacy and get on with their duties. Missing out on the closeness of family life is tough but married couples have many problems; he had listened to more than a few spill their hearts out in the confessional box over the years. Being unmarried means you have free mobility in order to be available to your parishioners without the burden of wife and children. This enables the priest to have full interest in his parish. Chris said a priest's life is also about moving around, which results in friendships being hard to sustain. He said it would have been a financial burden and that, had he been allowed to marry, he probably wouldn't have been able to give his wife a good life. I reminded him that married Anglican priests seem to manage perfectly well but he retorted that he didn't know how they financially managed.

Some say that since its introduction, celibacy has remained for many priests the pebble in their shoe. That's not to say that many relationships have not been formed. Some priests, especially attractive ones, were unable to maintain repression of their desires and conducted romances in secret, albeit often in fear of being caught. These liaisons often ended in heartache when the priests refused to leave the priesthood for their lovers.

Of course, celibacy and the Catholic Church's attitude towards sex, especially the Irish Church, needs to be remembered for its puritanical stance towards all kinds of sex, even in marriages, and to add to this absurdity was their stance towards contraception within marriages. Most anything to do with the body was considered bad and sinful — including indulging in any type of genital pleasure, risking damnation in the afterlife.

The debate around celibacy is more prevalent today than at any other time in the history of the Irish Church, especially considering the aging priesthood and lack of vocations. Psychologists have spoken out and deemed celibacy an unnatural state which goes against basic human instincts and thus causes emotional dysfunction in a person.

Yet, despite these findings — and various writings and protests among the clergy themselves — the curia steadfastly refuses to lift the ban, despite married Anglican priests being allowed to convert and join the Catholic priesthood. How much more evidence is required for the curia to realise the world is now too far advanced in psychology, sexuality and spirituality to consider this a healthy option? Many feel that priests of the future will want to get married and have children. It is estimated that a large percent of the Irish population believe that priests should be allowed to marry. However, as you will read later, this is unlikely to happen anytime soon.

▼ ▼ ▼

As part of my research for this book I visited a married priest so as to find out what life is like for a married priest in the Catholic Church, as well as to form (in general) a vision of what life could be like for married priests. Fr Kevin, who is in his early sixties, lives in London and was formerly an Anglican priest, before converting. After showing me around the adjoining church, we went into the parochial house where Kevin lived with his wife and the youngest of his three grown-up daughters. We sat in the living room, which was cosy and welcoming, and over wine he started telling me about his journey into the priesthood. The end part of St John's Gospel helped him make up his mind up about joining the Catholic priesthood; the part where it says, 'take me where you go — what are you doing here?' Kevin said that from a young age he had found his spiritual lift in life and from then onwards knew that he wanted to be a priest. His father had joked to people and said that there were worse things in life which could have happened and that Fr Kevin could have become a criminal instead. However, just before leaving the Anglican Church to convert to Catholicism and its priesthood, Kevin said he knew in his heart that he was already a Catholic, because from the age of 13 he had felt the faith and had grown fond of Romanish customs. He also said that he knew many Anglicans on the extreme edge of Catholicism. They know their church was constructed through an act of political history — by secular law — and that the Catholic Church is not an accident of political history. He said there were fewer people in this category opposed to the ordination of women priests than is publicly acknowledged and there is also a growing number of Anglicans who would encourage discussion regarding reconciliation with the Catholic Church when the issues of lifting celibacy and ordination of women priests bears fruition.

Kevin then proceeded to tell me about the ironic story in his parish of a priest who left the priesthood to get married and how he now attended mass with his wife every week. Kevin said that whenever he and the former priest met, they were friendly and gracious to each other but he remarked how this man, who he described as "a lovely man — a true priest", had his training wasted after being made to leave the priesthood owing to the outmoded rules on celibacy. In his mind, had this man been allowed to marry, he would still be a serving priest. This led us to discussing celibacy with the married priest mentioning how he often wondered where some Catholic priests channel their sexual energy, especially during their younger years. He then added, that from a married Anglican priest's point of view it is almost inconceivable how they manage without sex and intimacy in their lives. He wonders if elderly priests ever feel bitterness at their being denied a partner and children — and thus question if their vocation was worth it.

Kevin told me about an old man whose wife had just died. He visited the man at home and was instantly struck by the tears in his eyes. It was the middle of the day and the old man offered him a glass of whiskey and although he didn't feel like having a drink, he accepted it as he knew the old man wanted to share with him his sorrow. Kevin listened and said he understood the pain of the old man and could empathise with how he felt after losing his wife who he had been married to for fifty years. The point of the story was to do with a question as to how an unmarried priest could truly understand how the old man felt in his grief — given that such a priest would never have shared a profound intimacy with a spouse.

Kevin was scathing towards his Catholic colleagues who were unmarried. He described how he found many to be socially inept and awkward around women, before adding that most were terrible cooks who had to eat out most of the time. He also referred to the isolation and loneliness encountered by single priests who socialise infrequently, even among other members of the clergy. Kevin said the problem with priests is they don't see other priests say Mass and often get into a rut in both their ministry and private lives.

The Catholic Church in general is at a tipping point — and many had hoped Pope Francis would permit priests in the Amazon basin to marry, owing to the chronic shortage of priests in the area — but disappointingly such an experiment was not given the go-ahead. But if Pope Francis had given his permission, the rest of the world might have followed suit with similar trials — maybe even in Ireland too, given the number of aging priests and few available replacements? Ireland is very capable of change and many feel there would be little trouble embracing the lifting of celibacy, or indeed accepting the ordination of women priests, but for now such policies are not even at the proposal stage. The Vatican remains resistant to such widespread changes. Accusations of misogyny linger. Inequality among the sexes remains firmly in place, with women still viewed as inferior to men in the church. Until reform occurs at the very top of the hierarchy, there is simply little chance that the Irish Church will be able to introduce or lead on these issues.

▼ ▼ ▼

The debate of whether women should be ordained into the priesthood is contentious and the mere mention of it is met with anger and chastisement by the Vatican who are loath to enter any meaningful debate around the subject. Of course, there is no valid reason why women cannot be ordained into the Catholic Church because there is nothing in scripture which prevents it. Historians will even point to examples of the early church when women were fully ordained ministers. But despite the dwindling congregations, lack of vocations and the fact that in 5–10 years' time the vast majority of today's priests will be over 65, the Vatican remain in defiance over the issue. In times such as this, it is like the church resembles a sinking ship (such as RMS Titanic) with thousands of passengers on board. However instead of attempting to use every rescue method possible to prevent the ship sinking, and those on board from perishing, the church hierarchy would seemingly rather let it sink than put a salvage package in place — i.e. allow a female captain to take over and steer the ship safely to shore. The truth is that a growing number of Irish Catholics, including priests, feel that women should be allowed into the priesthood and that they would bring compassion, wisdom and progress into the church rather than add to its continuous decline.

It is noteworthy to consider that there are women in society who feel they have a vocation to the priesthood. These women want to be able to say Mass and administer the sacraments. They are not interested in other roles within the church and genuinely feel a calling towards the priesthood. This contrasts with believing that women haven't considered the possibility of priesthood or that women will only be able to consider vocations if the Vatican were to reverse their decision about women being ordained. I met one man, Tom, who told me how his wife, Veronica, has had a life-long desire to be a priest. She felt a strong sense of vocation from an early age. Veronica has gone through episodes of great upset to the point of going to bed crying that her desire for priesthood may never become a reality. She has spent her life calling for the ordination of women and the lifting of male celibacy. If her wish was granted this would see a model of priesthood like the Anglican Church that allows marriage and the ordination of men and women to their priesthood. In other words, Veronica could join the priesthood and remain married to Tom, who says he would be quite happy remaining a lay person but would be more than willing to support his wife.

The Catholic Church has a long history of not listening to women and Catholicism is not unlike the other two major world religions — Judaism and Islam — when it comes to accusations of treating women unfavourably to men. Some blame St Paul for being a misogynist who destroyed the role of women in the church, while others pinpoint this malaise towards the very beginning of humankind with its origins rooted in the Adam and Eve story. Eve is perpetually portrayed as the temptress who seduced Adam and whose sin brought shame and destruction upon mankind, preventing automatic entry to paradise after death. Stamped in its DNA, the church views women as weak and lustful and prone to leading men astray. This has allowed them to justify, albeit covertly, the way unmarried mothers were treated up until the 1980s. Their preoccupation with sex and women has meant that unmarried fathers were rarely, if ever, deemed sinful or told to repent in the way women were instructed. Catholics, particularly in the Irish Church, show great reverence towards Our Lady, and the clergy were encouraging of this because Our Lady was seen to be a virgin and pure of sin — thus this is what they expected all women to emulate. How procreation was supposed to advance wasn't discussed as this too would lead to other bones of contention within the church — namely contraception, which I mentioned earlier in the book.

The only role close to resembling a female priest in the Catholic Church is that of a nun. Their numbers have continued to dwindle radically since the 1960s with few now joining. There are currently less than two thousand nuns in Ireland and most of these are now in their seventies, eighties or older. I spoke to one nun in Knock, Sr Mary, who was in her seventies. Mary spoke frankly about how religious life was very hard in the 1960s when she joined. She recalled the long habits they wore and how they were instructed to stare at the ground and never look up and talk to people. Life in convents was extremely difficult. Most days there was only porridge for lunch and having food items like cheese and marmalade at weekends was considered a luxury. Mary feels a lot of falsehoods are being alleged about the past. She believed that some nuns, a small percentage, committed evil acts against others, but believes history must be willing to consider such events in their correct context and perspective. Mary referred to the sterling work nuns did, which frequently entailed raising up to fifteen babies in cramped living accommodation. There was minimal help from the state, and little was known at the time about sexual abuse in families (which also resulted in pregnancy).

These days, only a small trickle of young women join the nunhood in Ireland each year, combined with new religious orders coming from overseas. However, Mary doesn't believe that the ordination of women priests is the answer to the crisis in the Irish Church. She said she considered women who want to be priests are sometimes feminists or anti-men or hold a grievance towards male priests. Mary also spoke of women wanting to be priests as being wounded in their sexuality and want to get back at the church. She felt some of these women lack gentleness and warmth and failed to recognise that the church wants mother figures to be at the heart of its home, like a domestic household. Mary believes that the church holds roles for men and women, but the priesthood is best served by men. Mary said the main role of nuns these days is to bring love into a loveless society and added that love is what Catholicism should be about, seeing the dignity of the human person and seeing Jesus in every person. Mary believes in the five 'A's' — attention, acceptance, affection, appreciation and affirmation — which she feels should be extended to every person. The role of nuns in schools and hospitals has dwindled and shifted towards family homes, where younger nuns visit families and children where they teach people how to pray as well as educate people more on the Catholic faith.

When I asked Fr Seamus, an elderly priest, what he thought would be the long-term legacy of nuns in Ireland, he started the discussion by telling me how up until the 1970s priests could not hear a nun's confession without a grill being between them. One day a nun called to his house unexpectedly and wanted the priest to hear her confession. The only problem was that he was new to the parish and had no grill set up in the parochial house. Seamus thought fast for a solution and decided to use the spare wheel of a bicycle as a makeshift barrier! He howled with laughter as he recounted the story. On a more serious note he told me that nuns do not get good media coverage in Ireland, with the reaction often being derogatory towards them in light of stories relating to The Magdalene Laundries (exploitation of women in mother and baby homes) and the Tuam babies scandal (where hundreds of babies were buried in mass graves, including some in a septic tank). However, despite these cruel and gruesome events, Seamus said people failed to understand that it was only a percentage of nuns who did wrong and not whole communities.

Unfortunately, a small number did present with a pathology, resulting in perversion and cruelty after their sexual desires came out in misguided and inappropriate ways. Like priests, they had no sexual experience and were never made party to any knowledge, education, discussion or conversation that involved sexuality. Like priests, they were often lonely and isolated and being devoid of any form of intimacy they were starved of their humanness. Yet many remained truly human and devoted to the good of the church. In that respect, history might recall them as being more sinned against than sinning.

Their many good deeds should not be forgotten. There are those who feel the story of nuns needs to be re-written for people to realise how kind most of them were. Nuns were pioneers in setting up schools and hospitals, thereby changing the lives of so many Irish people for the better. Some say they were the feminists of their day — strong women — and champions for helping the poor. Many were 'heroines' in their communities, who looked after the deprived as well as providing an enormous service to hospitals, schools and orphanages — almost always without seeking publicity. Unlike many priests and the Catholic hierarchy, they were not afraid of helping during the early days of the AIDS epidemic and often showed great kindness and humanity.

Some experts predict that the next scandal to befall the Catholic Church will be revelations about the sexual abuse of nuns by priests. Sex abuse is alleged to have taken place in India, the Philippines and in various European countries including France, Italy and Ireland. But the spotlight is primarily on African countries where priests have been accused of asking nuns to be available for sex (so they would not risk contracting AIDS from local women) and of organising abortions for nuns they have impregnated.

▼▼▼

Amongst the dying church, life goes on for priests up and down the country. Those who are left, try to do their best for their parishioners. Fr Brendan lives in Dublin and is in his early sixties. He told me that he liked his congregation to share stories during his sermon. His parish had seen twenty gang-fuelled murders in the last decade. Brendan presided over many funeral Masses when the killer was known to be present. I attended a Saturday evening Mass in his church which contained a congregation of thirty-four people including myself.

Over tea and biscuits in his house afterwards, Brendan told me that storytelling had proved popular in the working-class parish whose worshippers often experienced exclusion and poverty. Some of the stories included the one about Sarah who told how one of her daughters set up home with a black partner. She was apprehensive about this at first, but he turned out to be the nicest of all her sons-in-law, which thereby demonstrated that he helped her to overcome prejudice towards black people. Then there was Anne whose son was gay. Her husband asked her if there was any pill that he could take to cure him! But the moral of the story was that Anne accepted her son's sexuality, as did the rest of the family, and eventually her husband did the same. Then there was Veronica whose daughter married a Muslim. Her daughter wasn't a practising Catholic but when she had a baby said that she would like to have her child baptised but not in a church. So, they decided to do their own impromptu baptism in their kitchen sink. This story caused much laughter in the church with Veronica telling the congregation that her Muslim son-in-law even joined them in the ceremony!

Then there was the time when Brendan delivered a sermon entitled 'The Bread of Life' and asked his parishioners what these words meant to them. A well-known traveller in the congregation shared his thoughts by saying that to him it meant looking at the sky and seeing how the birds fly, admiring the strength of the hills around him, noticing the insects on the ground and seeing his shadow when the sun shines brightly, before looking at his wife, Mary, mother of their ten children, and saying how he admired her for putting up with him. He concluded how they often laughed, argued and cried together and that was the way God found them.

Brendan said these were great revelations of wisdom for him because they embodied the incarnation of the godliness of life which is missing in the current priesthood. He referred to fellow

priests as bachelors who miss out on the 'messes' that most other
people experience. They are denied a better understanding of what
life is about because they aren't grounded in the mess of everyday
life.

Brendan ended our conversation by telling me about the
poem 'Gratitude' by Mary Oliver and how its positive message
should be part of the narrative of our lives to help bring meaning to
God and the world around us. It is important to question what we
hear, see and admire, what astonishes us and what we would like to
see again. It is also important to remind ourselves about the tenderness of life and appreciate its mystery and wonder. As you will read
in Oliver's poem, the essence of life is always around us and, often,
right in front of our eyes — yet we choose to not see it. The poem
reminds of the tenderness in life, and encourages us to think about
the world in terms of mystery and wonder.

What did you notice?
> The dew-snail;
> the low-flying sparrow;
> the bat, on the wind, in the dark;
> big-chested geese, in the V of sleekest performance;
> the soft toad, patient in the hot sand;
> the sweet-hungry ants;
> the uproar of mice in the empty house;
> the tin music of the cricket's body;
> the blouse of the goldenrod.

What did you hear?
> The thrush greeting the morning;
> the little bluebirds in their hot box;
> the salty talk of the wren,
> then the deep cup of the hour of silence.

When did you admire?
> The oaks, letting down their dark and hairy fruit;
> the carrot, rising in its elongated waist;

the onion, sheet after sheet, curved inward to the pale
green wand;
at the end of summer the brassy dust,
the almost liquid beauty of the flowers;
then the ferns, scrawned black by the frost.

What astonished you?
The swallows making their dip and turn over the water.

What would you like to see again?
My dog: her energy and exuberance, her willingness,
her language beyond all nimbleness of tongue,
her recklessness, her loyalty, her sweetness,
her strong legs, her curled black lip, her snap.

What was most tender?
Queen Anne's lace, with its parsnip root;
the everlasting in its bonnets of wool;
the kinks and turns of the tupelo's body;
the tall, blank banks of sand;
the clam, clamped down.

What was most wonderful?
The sea, and its wide shoulders;
the sea and its triangles;
the sea lying back on its long athlete's spine.

What did you think was happening?
The green beast of the hummingbird;
the eye of the pond;
the wet face of the lily;
the bright, puckered knee of the broken oak;
the red tulip of the fox's mouth;
the up-swing, the down-pour, the frayed sleeve
of the first snow—
so, the gods shake us from our sleep.

▼ ▼ ▼

I spoke to several of the priests I interviewed about confessions. I was interested to know if people still participated in this ritual that was once enshrined firmly in Irish Catholicism. In the past, people were encouraged to regularly attend confessions, no matter how trivial their sins. The worst thing that could happen to a person was to die not having confessed a mortal sin. In Ireland, mortal sin mainly involves sex. Confessions in Ireland have waned considerably since the 1980s with fewer people now attending on a regular basis except the elderly and most devout; however, Fr Padraic told me how he recently spent a morning in a Midlands secondary school hearing confession for teenagers from junior to senior levels. To his astonishment, more young people approached the ritual than he expected and had a reverence that surprised him. This example aside, the reality is less people are attending confession because, according to other priests I interviewed, there is a loss of sense of sin these days. Sins, like theft from the workplace, are easily justified by saying that everybody else is doing it and, therefore, it becomes normalised and not considered sinful behaviour. But the most prevalent factor as to why confession attendance is in decline is because people no longer hold rigid views about sex being sinful. Liberation bloomed in this respect and by the mid-eighties the church had finally lost power and control on this matter, which was later reinforced in the nineties by several scandals involving clergy members, including a prominent Irish bishop, having had children while remaining in the priesthood. This hypocrisy was not well received by the wider Irish society.

Changing views on sex is not to say that some of the older clergy won't still preach or comment on sexual sins, although this is now quite rare, but when I mentioned this to one priest in his late seventies he told me about a couple and their young child who had come to him to ask to get married, resulting in him making his feelings known. He said he remarked to them, "is this the right way around?", pointing to their child. According to him, priests are frightened to mention anything that makes them unpopular and therefore no longer preach about sin and its consequences. In

Chris' view the devil is winning fast, but he doesn't think this is the fault of the church.

In the past, priests preached about the sins of the body and how, when used for wrongful acts, this would result in eternal damnation. The seed of fear was planted firmly and repeatedly in confessions right up until the eighties. Up until then, priests considered sex, sexual desires and masturbation as mortal sins, but gradually over the years there has been a softening of views, although official church teachings on the subject of sex remain intact.

Fr Hugh, who is in his mid-fifties, mentioned the importance of the church not condemning or being over-judgemental because priests themselves come from families and everybody has their own stories to tell. He said this in relation to priests having gay family members and relatives who are divorced. I read out a list and asked him if he thought any of the acts on my list were sins and enquired of his views. Most of his answers, with the exception of the one about abortion, showed hesitancy and lacked conviction. This illustrated how at odds individual priests are in their own personal views compared to the stance the church takes in matters of sin and morality. These were the questions on my list:

Is masturbation a sin?
"Yes — but people shouldn't lose any sleep over it."

Are homosexual acts a sin?
"Yes, sinful, yet there are worse things a person could do provided their intentions are mitigated by commitment rather than promiscuity whereby they are not abusing a gift."

Is sex before marriage in heterosexuals a sin?
"Sinful but with a small 's' because couples these days nearly always live together before they get married. Families are accepting of this provided the couple are committed to each other."

Is divorce a sin?

"No, the church wouldn't like to see people living in a bad situation — at risk of violence. Remarriage, though, is a sin."

Is same sex marriage a sin?

"Sinful with a small 's'. This should not come to marriage which should be exclusively between a man and a woman."

Is abortion a sin?

"Sinful, I abhor abortion even in cases of rape and incest because I always think about couples who are unable to have children."

Most of the priests I spoke to told me that hearing confessions these days takes a much different format than that of yesteryear and is far more relaxing and informal. Sometimes, it is more of a conversation or informal counselling and guidance. It is no longer carried out exclusively in the traditional sense of the church confessional box with the rigid 'Bless me Father for I have sinned' mantra being played out. It can often take place during a private meeting with a priest. Frequently, a priest begins the meeting by asking the penitent what they want to thank God for before asking what the things are that worry them.

People still reach out to priests during times of crisis and uncertainty. Most priests I spoke to said they much preferred this new way of interacting with people and felt that the old type of confessions is not worth remedying because people were fearful of being honest due to the power imbalance between priest and penitent. Whether the Vatican approves of this new method is unclear although the rules for a priest giving absolution remain in place. Debate about the meaning of people's conscience was noticeable during the abortion and same-sex referendums, with some arguing that a person can be of good conscience despite voting 'yes' in opposition to the church's stance. Some bishops condemned Catholics who voted in contradiction to church teachings and recommended confessions

to seek absolution for sinful behaviour. Others thought it wrong
that bishops condemned like this without considering that a person's conscience is between the person and God. The only thing
that is clear in Ireland is that the confessional format of decades
gone by is truly consigned to the history books, except for the occasional elderly priest who refuses to change or the elderly penitent
who had adhered to this practice all their lives.

As you will have read in this book so far, the changes in Ireland
over the past thirty years have been unexpected and unprecedent-
ed. You will also discover in the next few chapters that the Irish
Church will either see further decline in the direction of extinction
or it will reform and rebirth itself into a new church where a more
tolerant and generous form of Catholicism will emerge. There are
a few other possibilities that I will expand upon later in the book,
but the church for now limps on through loss, fear, grief, anger and
disgust. When — or if — hope and joy enter the equation, remains
to be seen.

Gay Priests

This is my commandment, that you love one another
as I have loved you.
(Jesus)
John 12:15

Pope Francis is liked by many Catholics and non-Catholics alike. It's easy to see why. He is a humble and friendly person who wants to do a good job in the reform of the church. He has requested that priests work hard and should smell of sheep by going out into their communities, working with ordinary people and being part of their trials and joys in everyday life. However, he is old, and he knows that his time is limited. There is much to be done in the church to repair and reform in the aftermath of the last few decades of clerical sexual abuse and the overall general decline in church attendances and adherence to the faith. Despite Pope Francis' positive points, when it comes to the issue of homosexuality he seems to regress intellectually and show character not unlike other high ranking and homophobic members of the Catholic hierarchy. He has made several hurtful remarks about the LGBT community — such as: there is no place for gay priests in the clergy — and following his trip to Ireland in 2018 he was heard to say that gay children should be taken to see a psychiatrist. Although previously he said that if somebody was gay, was searching for the Lord and has goodwill, then who was he to judge. Did he include gay priests in this, I wonder?

There are currently over 400,000 Catholic priests in the world (nearly 4,000 in Ireland) and based on the anecdotal premise that at least 60 percent are gay, does this mean that Pope Francis wants over 200,000 to pack their suitcases and leave the priesthood? Does Pope Francis, who appears to be less of an emperor pope than his predecessors, hold a rigid and ignorant view that confuses homosexuality and paedophilia? Does he subscribe to the church's official stance that practising homosexuals are intrinsically disordered? Does he belief there are 'gay' cures and therapies which 'reverse' homosexuals into heterosexuals? Surely, this kind and intelligent man cannot be that ignorant and misguided? There is evidence he can come across sometimes as being inconsistent. He previously opposed same-sex marriage and gay adoption but spoke out strongly in favour of civil unions and equal rights for homosexuals. Paul Vallely, in his book, *Pope Francis: Untying the Knots*, mentioned how aware he is of the gay lobby within the Vatican and knows about its active gay networks, blackmail and corruption. Therefore, it is safe to conclude that Pope Francis is neither uneducated nor in the dark, but his grasp of how the Catholic Church should adequately address the issue of homosexuality and gay clergy remains unsteady.

When I mentioned to Fr Jack, a priest I interviewed, that the pope made remarks about not wanting gay men to join the priesthood he laughed heartily before saying that this was a classic example of locking the barn door after the horse has bolted. He said it's nonsense because the church is "full of homosexual priests at every level of the church". Jack told me a story about how he was out walking his dog one night when he started a conversation with a young man aged around twenty-five. It was a brief and pleasant conversation about dogs. After bidding goodnight, the young man nodded to the church and said to Jack how he would never go inside. Jack asked him the reason why and the young man replied that he was gay. Jack was accepting of this but before departing said to the young man that for whatever it was worth, he would be always be welcome inside while he was the priest in charge. Two weeks later he noticed the young man at Mass with another young man. After Mass was over, Jack stood outside the church and was greeting parishioners as they left when the young man and his friend came over to say hello. The young man introduced his companion to Jack as his partner before commenting on how they liked the sermon and music. Jack said that perhaps they saw how unfazed he was that they were a same-sex couple attending Mass that led to the young man telling him he wanted to ask him a question. He asked Jack whether he would have refused them communion, had they gone up to receive it. Jack's response to them confirmed that there wasn't the slightest chance of him refusing. He explained to them that if he started refusing people communion where would he stop? Would he refuse unmarried heterosexual couples who were in sexual unions, or divorced people who had remarried? What about refusing those who had watched porn or those who masturbated regularly and so on? What if he denied communion to those who voted 'yes' in the various referendums over the years contrary to what the church had asked? If that was to be the criteria the church rigidly set, Jack asked the two young men at what point would the priest himself be turned away if such strict guidelines were enforced?

It is estimated that there is a disproportionate number of homosexuals in the priesthood with estimates placed at 60 percent gay, 20 percent heterosexual and the remaining 20 percent confused about their sexuality. Donald Cozzens, in his book, *The Changing Face of the Priesthood,* reflected on American Catholic priests and concluded that anywhere from 23 to 58 percent of American Catholic clergy were gay. Cozzens also pointed out that throughout the history of the Catholic Church, many priests, bishops and even popes and saints have been homosexual. Frédéric Martel, in his book, *In the Closet of the Vatican: Power, Homosexuality, Hypocrisy,* stated that 80 percent of the Vatican's top clerics are gay. With gay priests, a distinction might be made between those who are 'practising' or 'non-practising', in respect to homosexuality. Some priests maintain privacy in their life and will not intentionally present as having a heterosexual identity, which makes it difficult to discern whether they are gay or not. There are others less guarded who will be satisfied with having gay inclinations and neither deny nor confirm their identity. Then there are those who practise and remain unbothered about their lifestyle being known. There are also some gay priests who have partners, but keep their relationship hidden from view.

There appears to be a disproportionate number of gay men training to be priests with indications showing figures to be well above the national average. What is it about the priesthood that attracts them? Are they more nurturing, sensitive and empathetic than heterosexuals, which ultimately are qualities suited for the priesthood? Or is it because they can live life without suspicion being raised about their sexuality? Despite this there is still strong denial from the Vatican which reaffirms the notion that homosexuality should not be taken into the seminary — yet people know there is a long-standing presence of homosexuality amongst Catholic priests.

There has been several rumours and allegations of homosexual activity both at St Patrick's, the national seminary in Maynooth, and in the Pontifical Irish College, Rome, during the past few years. This includes media reporting about seminarians being found in bed together in both seminaries — and how some seminarians at Maynooth were using Grindr, a gay dating app. However, internal inquiries found that these allegations were unproven and were the result of anonymous letters being sent to the media allegedly by an internal source. However, the allegations did not prevent senior Irish clerics, including the Archbishop of Dublin, from from commenting that there was a worrying atmosphere at the seminary in Maynooth in the aftermath of the claims. I have since heard of a curious atmosphere at St Patrick's whereby the sexual identity of seminaries are constantly questioned, rather than the focus being on their understanding and ability to keep the vow of celibacy.

▼ ▼ ▼

Cardinal Ratzinger (later Pope Benedict XVI) and the Congregation of the Doctrine of the Faith issued one of the first documents on homosexuality entitled, 'On the Pastoral Care of Homosexual Persons' in 1986 (which was approved by Pope John Paul II). Prior to this the church was primarily silent on the issue and this was the first time the Vatican attempted to address the issue of homosexuals (lesbians were not mentioned). Up until then the church was only concerned with 'deviant sexual behaviour' and considered all sexual acts (including masturbation) outside of heterosexual marriage to be mortally sinful. In this new document, Ratzinger argued it was wrong to claim that the homosexual orientation was either good or neutral and basically advocated against public opinion being formed whereby homosexual acts could be condoned or become acceptable. He concluded that in doing so the church and society would become powerless in preventing what was considered as moral disorder, and while homosexuals were not evil people they tended to be drawn towards being intrinsically and morally evil by their sexual acts. Perhaps, Ratzinger forgot to look more closely at historical matters closer to home.

Cardinal John Henry Newman, who was canonised a saint in 2019, is perhaps one of the best-known gay priests in history. Newman was probably the most famous Catholic theologian of the late 19th century. Ordained as an Anglican priest, he studied and taught at Oxford University before his conversion to Roman Catholicism in 1845. He is known to have had a deep emotional relationship with another priest, Fr Ambrose St. John, who he met in Rome where they both studied theology. They were inseparable and lived together. So intense was their love for each other, they requested to be buried in the same grave together. In many ways, John and Ambrose were light years ahead of their time.

There are many questions that the church is unable to answer; the first being what difference, if any, does the sexual orientation of a man have on his ability to be a priest? How would the laity respond to having an openly gay priest in their community? I will return to this point later in this chapter. Thirdly, would being gay affect a gay priest's ability to perform his duties around families and children? Bearing in mind gay people can be found in almost every other profession in the world, why then should it not automatically be the case with priests? It doesn't affect social workers, doctors, nurses, police, teachers and others who work with children.

Is homosexuality really a growing phenomenon in the priesthood or are we simply more aware of it now than in past generations? The quick answer to this is to recognise that homosexuality in the priesthood is not something new. In mainstream society, up until the 1990s, homosexuality was considered promiscuous partly because of the AIDS epidemic so there was a resistance and a discomfort among gay priests who were inwardly torn about their own sexuality. Even to the current day, gay priests are torn with the church's moral convictions on the subject.

It is inevitable that many gay individuals are in the clergy; however, the church remains unsure how to deal with the issue — and so they remain in denial. Lives are therefore conducted in intense secrecy, with very few priests 'coming out', although some might have close friends they confide in or they travel to the UK, Italy or America to attend confidential retreats for gay priests. I have spoken to an Irish priest living in the UK who facilitates retreats for gay priests, and among the attendees are gay priests from Ireland who come over especially to unwind and be themselves in a safe and caring environment. It is said gay priests form intimate relationships more easily than straight priests — because it is easier for gay priests to have male friends, than for heterosexual priests to have female friends (given this leads to innuendo and gossip).

It is necessary to recognise that Ireland, until a few decades ago was a repressed society. Even on TV chat shows, speaking about sex made people feel ill at ease. The majority of people were negative about homosexuality until about 30 years ago, though attitudes have changed relatively quickly since then. Unfortunately, the church hasn't kept up with the pace of this social change. There remains a reluctance to acknowledge that people have moved beyond messages which stated that being gay is bad, wrong and evil. The church still struggles to come to terms with the little power they hold over people's morality which was been reshaped by sources outside the church. Therefore, the best outcome for most gay priests (who are content with their sexual orientation) is for the church to state that it is acceptable for them to remain in the priesthood providing they remain faithful to their promise of celibacy. It also seems preferable that priests remain discreet and not discuss their homosexuality with colleagues or parishioners. There are of course a few gay priests who are celibate but are open about their sexuality and willing to discuss it.

▼▼▼

I met with an openly gay priest in a Dublin parish who came out to his congregation during the time of the same sex referendum in 2015. Fr Robert expressed his views and told people at

Mass one Saturday evening that he would be voting 'yes' because he was gay himself. He made it clear, in case anybody had any confusion in the aftermath of the clerical sex abuse scandals, that he had no interest in children. The reception from his congregation consisted of widespread support both verbally and silently. Robert's ministry hasn't suffered as a result of his announcement with Mass attendance in his church remaining the same. However, not everybody was delighted by his disclosure and shortly afterwards his bishop summoned him for a meeting. Robert knew he had done nothing wrong. He said people in Ireland had remained silent far too long about many issues, and therefore couldn't fully 'be themselves'. Robert added that he disliked how priests in Ireland always seemed to be on the other side to that of the people. He now wanted to stand on the same level as everybody else. He would no longer pretend to be somebody he wasn't. For him, the days of regression were over, and he disliked the way the bishop summoned him to be reprimanded like a naughty school child. Robert informed the bishop's secretary that he would come to see him at his own convenience. He was determined that he wouldn't lose his job as a result of his sexual orientation. Being celibate he knew he had Canon Law on his side and made this known to the bishop when they eventually met. Robert added that, overall, he had a better reaction from ordinary people than from church authorities, including fellow priests who remained silent on the subject when they met him. He felt his parishioners now see and hear him as his true self — both as a person and priest. Robert went on to say that the church fails to understand the complexities of life, especially as regards to how sexual identification and celibacy is a problem for priests. And that avoiding discussing these issues, denies them their true significance and importance.

When I attended one of Robert's weekend Masses, his sermon was entitled, 'Who do you say I am?' which proved to be one of the most uplifting sermons I have ever heard a priest deliver. He spoke about Jesus being a brilliant 'psychologist' who loved spending time conversing with many diverse people — from whom he also learned much. Jesus didn't just perform miracles. Rather he lived amongst his people, encouraging and guiding them. He couldn't just remain silent and aloof. He made outsiders feel they belonged. Did Jesus not say, "You must love God with all your heart and soul — and you must love your neighbour as you love yourself?" Robert also spoke about the need for people to be true to themselves and know that God loves them even though the institutional church may tell them otherwise. He concluded his sermon by saying that one of the biggest problems is the church's wrongfulness in not making people feel like they belong.

Afterwards when we met in private, he also spoke about joining the priesthood in the 1970s and how nothing was ever spoken about sex or homosexuality. The only mention of homosexuality was in a lecture he attended on moral theology when the bishop delivering the lecture said that a good homosexual was comparable to a good alcoholic. The latter was good in the sense that they refrained from alcohol despite intense cravings to drink. Robert pointed out the often contradictory stance of the church when it preaches that homosexual acts are evil while on the other hand says, 'God created (all men) in his own image', before adding that the Catholic Church has also stifled discussion about Jesus' views on sexuality to suit its own needs. The most interesting thing about Jesus and the subject of homosexuality is that there is nothing recorded which says he ever mentioned it, least of all condemned it. There is absolutely nothing mentioned in the gospels about homosexuality. He also mentioned how we have no inkling of Jesus' sexuality and how he personally has often wondered if Jesus ever got married and had children because Judeans of that time believed in having children so that they could leave something behind.

▼▼▼

Many priests, in the past, had little insight into their own sexuality. Some discussed the subject as if it were 'outside' and separate of them. They spoke objectively — rather than subjectively. Many priests haven't dealt with their own sexuality because the church doesn't allow them to address this. Undoubtedly, this has had and continues to have a detrimental effect on their self-worth and emotional well-being. Fr John refused to accept my suggestion that the church preferred heterosexual priests to homosexual priests. He was adamant that the church wouldn't differentiate between either because all that mattered was that priests remain celibate. Was he saying they should remain silent about their sexual orientation, ignore the church's stance and the Vatican's officialdom — and everything will be fine? I continued in my attempt to have a discussion on the subject stating that in its current stance there is nothing welcoming for gay priests in the ministry and cited examples of church homophobia, however, John was unwilling to agree with me. I felt he was being intentionally obstinate and for a time I persisted in presenting my points until I eventually relented, sensing I was wasting my time. John could not or would not adequately express his personal views on homosexuality within the Catholic priesthood. I left the meeting with the feeling that I had encountered a man in denial of himself!

Fr Chris, on the other hand, was quite clear that he doesn't like the idea of homosexuals being in the priesthood. I cited the high statistics to him which suggest many Catholic priests are gay but, after shaking his head, he responded by saying he doesn't believe them. Then he proclaimed that priests have strength and commitment, and that they avoid homosexuality because of their love of Jesus. Chris said he has never discussed homosexuality with priest friends. He would find it an embarrassing subject but if any priest or parishioner told him they were gay (none had during his ministry), he would ask them to consider if they felt it truly the correct thing for them. Chris denied that he rejects gay people or that he is homophobic, rather it a case of him not liking *what* they are as opposed to *who* they are. He had no feeling towards AIDS victims and didn't feel the Catholic Church had a duty to show kindness towards the earlier victims of the disease in the eighties. He said his parishioners didn't expect to be addressed on this subject,t before saying that God did not make anybody homosexual. Instead, he feels everybody is given choices in life and it is the duty of a priest to remind them of that, help them decide how best to avoid temptation, and give reminders about the teachings of the church on homosexuality!

Nowadays, priests are gradually beginning to talk about sexuality, celibacy and their own personal lives, including homosexuality. It was not until the 1980s that society, including priests themselves, considered the possibility that gay men joined the priesthood, so naive were they about sexuality in general. It is therefore not surprising that in past generations, the policy of 'don't ask — don't tell' was applied to men entering the priesthood. However, it is remarkable that such is still the norm today. But today's world is different. There is increasing openness about the subject, together with a growing awareness in mainstream society of the prevalence of gay clergy. Whether the church chooses to acknowledge this, however, is another matter.

Fr Brian, another openly gay priest, told me that when young men entered seminaries in the past, sexual maturity was never a consideration and that none were educated and/or counselled towards a healthy understanding of their sexuality. Celibacy was the only thing on offer and even that was seldom discussed. A sexless, chaste life was just expected to be taken for granted. Brian said the priesthood acts as a haven for those who are fearful of their sexuality. It is a retreat to a safe place of their own construction (both for younger and older candidates). As well as being an escape route from internal non-acceptance of their sexuality, the priesthood allows them to become part of a community and give them something to identify with. Fr Brian said that gay people can often be drawn towards things of God. They envisage lives where they are intermediaries between God and the people.

Is the priesthood edging towards it being okay for new recruits to openly admit to being gay but choose to be celibate? There is no evidence of this because the church remains totally secretive and retains a cruel and harsh stance on homosexuality, which they maintain is 'intrinsically' disordered. Therefore, is it reasonable to assume that any self-accepting gay man entering the Catholic priesthood becomes part of an institution that hates them? Brian added that self-accepting men entering the priesthood, who would openly admit they are gay (even if they said they were willing to be celibate), would not be treated the same as somebody who remained silent, was full of self-hatred owing to them battling internalised homophobia. It is correct, therefore, to garner the view that the wrong type of gay person often joins the priesthood and that it contains its fair share of men who remain confused, scared and angry about their sexuality.

Fr James Alison shares a similar view in an article he wrote in *The Tablet* in 2018 entitled, 'Homosexuality amongst the clergy: Caught in a trap of dishonesty' where he stated: 'It is closeted men who are the worse persecutors. Some are very sadly disturbed souls who cannot but try to clean outwardly what they cannot admit to being inwardly. These can't be helped since Church teaching reinforces their hell.' This is simply entrenched homophobia in the church, with fixed views that all gay people are promiscuous and that gay people in general are sinful — and further, that gay priests would be targets for blackmail. In cases of extreme ignorance (as already mentioned) there are some who think homosexuality and paedophilia are closely linked. It is sad that the church remains so backward thinking and that it is its own worst enemy in terms of hypocrisy and inhumanity that are contrary to the teachings of Jesus.

The former Pope Benedict, who was renowned for his homophobia and insensitive remarks about gay people, said in his 2008 Christmas message that saving humanity from homosexual or transsexual behaviour was just as important as saving the rainforest from destruction. During his pontificate, the Vatican called homosexuality 'a deviation, an irregularity, a wound'. However, during my research I discovered a piece of wisdom from him in his book entitled *Principles of Catholic Theology* (1987), which was written long before he became pope. While it is deeply theological in tone, its irony will not be lost on the LGBT community when he discusses how a person has to encounter love before they encounter morality before he asks the question, 'Who or what is an individual to like if he does not like himself?' Is this not a question that every gay priest who battles internalised homophobia should be asking themselves?

▼ ▼ ▼

I met several liberal priests who hold the view, in their ministry, that every person is equal in the eyes of God. Fr Kevin expressed things succinctly, saying:

> *"It doesn't matter if somebody is homosexual because God still loves them. If they are in a sexual relationship, God still loves them. If they try to stop, God still loves them. What if they can't stop? God still loves them."*

Kevin added that the tipping point for many is when one day they realise that some of the closest people in their lives, including family members and close friends, are gay. Often that moment of realisation becomes the turning point which results in a change in their homophobic attitudes. Kevin said if any homophobic priest were to sit down and hear an LGBT child tell their story, and really listen with compassion, then they would know they'd be moved enough to change the way they view LGBT people and indeed themselves. It will change the way they see things, and once such insight is gained a person is unlikely to discriminate ever again. Kevin asked how a priest can preach about what is or isn't God's will if you are saying that one part of God's creation is not as valid as another part? Are they preaching that God does not align homosexual love and make it as valid as any other type of love?

It is often said that those who are comfortable with their own sexual identity are not prone to homophobia, because then they are absent of doubt and don't feel threatened in their masculinity. Could this be equally true for heterosexual priests? Would they be more comfortable around the issue of homosexuality and find less reason to judge and discriminate? I considered this to be the case with Fr Dermot who stated that he is heterosexual. Another such like priest, Fr Martin, held liberal views and showed great humanity when recounting a story about an experience he had a few years ago. He was on holiday with family members in Cork and one evening, when they were walking back to their hotel, they came across three young adult men in their twenties. One of the young men was very upset, crying uncontrollably. His friends were doing their best to comfort him. Martin remembers his sister saying that she thought she overheard him say he had earlier come out to his father as a gay man and his father had become very angry. The other young men were just listening to their friend and holding him and trying to support him. Martin wondered what would have been next for him? What would the next meeting with his father and family be like? He thought to himself how the young man shouldn't have to suffer like that because family should be a haven where young people can find support and understanding. Martin hopes he found it and that the young man is being given love and support from his family and friends.

Another priest, Fr David, who was in his early sixties, confided that he was uncertain about his own sexuality. When I asked him if he thought homosexuality was a sin, he replied that it depended on the conscience of the individual. He said if he heard somebody's confession and they confessed to having sex with a member of their own sex, he would interpret this as them considering it a sin and therefore he would give the man absolution. Outside of the confessional box, it is up to the individual to determine whether they have committed a sin in this respect. But he added God's final judgement is His alone and it is not for priests or bishops to decide when somebody has sinned in this respect.

The church's teaching remains steadfast in the belief that any sex outside marriage is unacceptable. About homosexuals, the view is taken that any sex is disordered. This is based on the principle that doctrine is static and doesn't develop — i.e. interpretation of the Bible will never relate to contemporary ideas of sexuality and gender, even considering what society now knows about these issues in comparison to earlier centuries. Even those in loving committed relationships will find themselves shunned because the church finds same-sex expressions of love challenging, with their response mainly being one of condemnation. The church continues to use insulting and insensitive language more in line with St Augustine who was critical of homosexuality and compared it to the story of Sodom and morality in the Bible. In contrast, gay people inadvertently subscribe more to the teachings of St *Thomas Aquinas,* the revered Dominican priest, who said that any person who acted in contradiction to their nature was committing a sin.

There are signs, even in some traditional parishes, that the issue of homosexuality has become less contentious but this could just be due to newer legislation, under which prosecution can be brought for homophobia and hate speech. There are others who say it is connected to a 'pathological' silence by gay priests who themselves are battling internal homophobia and won't even allow themselves to discuss the subject. Homophobia from the church sometimes ignites parents more than their LGBT children. Parents, family and friends of LGBT people have either stood up and challenged priests during Mass or have walked out during negative sermons when discussing same-sex relationships and marriage. Devoted parents have retorted by saying that the church does not speak for the children they have raised — and who are loving individuals. Such outward declarations of support, illustrate that parents (and even grandparents) are accepting of the situation — and have dealt with the coming out of their children and grandchildren. The question, therefore, is why can't the church do the same? Personally, I would urge anybody who has a priest denounce homosexuality to ask the priest if he is gay himself — or question him on why he thinks there are so many gay priests in the Catholic Church.

Despite what I have written in this chapter about the high number of gay priests, the LGBT community largely remains invisible in the eyes of the church. Many gay Catholics feel unwelcomed, excluded and insulted once they disclose their identity. And it is not just gay men — lesbians and transgender people also feel their existence and individuality is unacknowledged and disrespected in this hostile atmosphere. Fr James Martin's book, *Building a Bridge,* looked at how the Catholic Church and the LGBT community need to end this contentious and combative struggle and become more warm and welcoming towards each other. The hypocrisy and divisiveness need to stop. The insensitive and homophobic language used by some priests and bishops — for example, using expressions like 'afflicted with same-sex attraction' which inadvertently includes some of their fellow priests — must end. The silliness and prejudice must cease before the church becomes even more farcical on this issue than at present. But among this abusive quagmire it is important for every LGBT person to remember who they really are, which is summed up beautifully in a prayer that appears in Martin's book: *Loving God, you made me who I am. I praise you and I love you, for I am wonderfully made, in your own image.*

Paedophile Priests

Let the one among you who is without
sin be the first to cast a stone.
(Jesus)
John 8:7

A small number of people, either through wilful ignorance or mis-conception, confuse homosexuality and paedophilia by thinking they are closely connected to each other. The clear distinction be-tween these is that gay people are not interested in having sex with children — the complete opposite to paedophiles. Gay people do not pursue relationships with anybody under the age of consent. Sexual activity between members of the same sex is by mutual con-sent with both partners over the age of consent. Paedophiles disre-gard the laws prohibiting sex with a child under the age of consent. Uppermost in their minds is their quest for sexual gratification with children. Their perverted pathology has led them to believe that such gratification can only be achieved via children. And so, it is with this impulse they pursue children — either male or fe-male — to satisfy their distorted desires. It goes without saying that because of their age, the vulnerable victims are never able to give informed consent.

Sexual abuse in families is phenomenally high, with one out of every four children becoming a victim at some point in their childhood. When analysing sexual abuse, it is noteworthy that the largest group of sex offenders in society are married men. Step-parents and children of their partner feature high in this. Child sexual abuse includes fondling the child or making a child touch the adult's genitals and/or involving the child in masturbation as well as penetration with an object, a finger or penis. Exposing genitals or making a child watch sex or look at pornographic pictures or involving the child in pornography are also predatory features of sexual abuse. One in eight girls and one in twelve boys are said to have been sexually abused before the age of sixteen. One in four girls and one in nine boys experience abuse in childhood and most of the abuse happens in the home with the perpetrator known to the victim.

Paedophilia is considered a psychiatric disorder in psychiatry's diagnostic manuals, where it is termed as 'paedophilic disorder'. It is defined as recurrent and intense sexual urges towards prepubescent children. For somebody to be diagnosed with paedophilia, they must be aged 16 years and be at least five years older than their victims (prepubescent children). A significant number of prepubescent boys were sexually abused by Catholic priests.

Another phenomena in the category of paedophilia is the disorder called 'ephebophilia,' which consists of primary interest in mid-to-late adolescents from the age of 15 upwards. A large percentage of paedophile priests committed their crimes against this age group. The victims were looked upon as no longer being children but not quite adults. It is noteworthy that classical Persian and Turkish literature often described adult men with erotic interest in adolescent males, which gave a degree of acceptance to this pathological condition.

Clerical sex abuse is far less widespread than the headlines suggest; however, over a thousand Irish priests have been accused of sexual offences against children. Nearly a hundred of these have been convicted and imprisoned for paedophilic acts with young boys and adolescents. These statistics alone indicate that nearly one in four Irish priests have been accused, implicated or convicted of sexual offences. Overall, it is estimated that between two and seven percent of Catholic priests worldwide are paedophiles based on the number convicted of sexual offences. It's not unusual, though, to read newspaper headlines or social media posts referring to articles where the previous Pope Benedict, as well as some cardinals, have made claims that sexual abuse in the church is to be blamed on the moral depravity of gays. It seems that they think this scapegoating will exonerate the abuse scandals that have blighted the church and restore innocence. The truth is, the reality of sexual identity is entirely separate from the problem of sexual abuse, because if this wasn't the case there would be higher numbers of paedophiles in the church, given the disproportionate number of gays in the priesthood. Furthermore, the John Jay College of Criminal Justice in New York conducted an independent study of sexual abuse in the priesthood from 1950 up to 2002 and confirmed that at no point did they find a connection between homosexual identity and an increased likelihood of sexual offending involving minors.

Based on this statistic, it is not possible to indicate or prove that the church is guiltier of sexual offences against children compared to wider society, given that we know most abuse — sexual and physical — takes place within the family context. The impression is often given through the media that child abuse is rife in the Catholic Church, which is untrue and grossly unfair. It must be highlighted there is no other institution, and no other Christian denomination or religion, which has been investigated by various authorities as thoroughly as the Catholic Church. So, there is no real comparison to any other organisation that has gone through such scrutiny. And even with professional groups there isn't any research that would cover, for example, schoolteachers, social workers, psychologists, doctors, police officers and sports trainers.

▼▼▼

Priests were put in positions where they were not answerable. They were put on pedestals. They were part of a closed organisation that was extremely secretive. But in fairness to the church, there is still puzzlement about paedophilia in the wider society. It was not until the late 1970s and early '80s when it was named and identified. A Jesuit priest I interviewed who studied psychology, philosophy, science, sociology and art during his seminary years mentioned how paedophilia never featured as a topic. Sex abuse scandals only surfaced in Ireland following scandals exposed in America and Australia. Brendan Smyth was the first clerical abuse scandal to come to public prominence in the 1990s — eventually revealing that over a period of 40 years the Belfast-born priest had abused up to 200 children. After this, more and more claims of sexual abuse were made against priests to the point that it shook the foundation of the church. As clerical abuse scandals erupted in Ireland, similar scandals unfolded in France, Germany and other countries in Europe. At one point, it seemed as if there was an 'outbreak' of paedophile priests across the world.

In the past, prior to the scandals erupting in Ireland, any sexual misconduct of priests reported to the gardai (police) was in turn referred to bishops — as situations of this sort were considered 'church matters', best dealt with in this manner. Furthermore, anybody who wrote to a bishop expressing concern about the inappropriate sexual behaviour of a priest resulted in them either receiving a polite reply or their letter was ignored, in the hope that no more would be heard about the matter. Up until the 1980s, bishops too would have known little about the manifestations of paedophilia, but I think this excuse, which to a degree was a valid reason for ignorance, garnered less merit in the succeeding years when paedophilia became more openly discussed in the media.

But cover-ups continued within the church and the abuse continued. In this sense the church adopted the same mentality of other institutions — they cover up their crimes in the hope they would never be discovered. It was only when a group of victims got together and found the strength to speak out, that action was taken. The righteous anger of the victims brought matters to public attention, which then led to many abusing priests being revealed. But the cover-up continued for many years afterwards, even when priests were imprisoned for sexual offences. The cover-ups only added shame to the church and more misery to the victims when a more forthright admission may have brought liberation to the church rather than cause further scandal. However, it is said that the bishops and the Vatican put various institutional self-interests first, and it is for this reason alone that the Catholic Church lied and bribed its way through the worst crisis it had faced in living memory. Pope Benedict was accused of making decisions to leave priests who had raped young boys unpunished — and, instead, merely transferring such priests to new dioceses, where they continued to find new victims.

People often wonder how the Catholic Church got it so wrong and never sought to fully remove abusing priests from a ministry which had access to children. Still nothing was done once paedophilia was given a name and society was aware of its existence, except for bishops to move abusing priests to a new parish after a period of contemplation and prayer. Unfortunately, prayers do not cure paedophilia. By nature, paedophiles are liars and extremely cunning and manipulative individuals. Priests were trusted. They held power and control and had easy access to children. But priests always had an immaturity when it came to sex. There was a 'jungle' of sexual energy floating about the priesthood at its height. Before examining the possible causes of paedophilia in the priesthood, I think it is first worth considering what psychotherapy offers as means of explanation in the mindset of abusing priests.

In psychoanalysis there are two terms used to best describe healthy and unhealthy formation in sexual maturity. Egosyntonic refers to the behaviours, values and feelings of a person that agree with or are acceptable to the needs and goals of the ego and therefore consistent with the person's ideal self-image in how they present to the world. Obviously, this is a healthy position to be in. An unhealthy frame of mind is described in psychoanalysis as being in a state of egodystonic. This refers to thoughts, compulsions and desires that conflict with the needs and goals of the ego, and is therefore inconsistent and in conflict with the person's ideal self-image. A paedophile's mind is forever in conflict with their personality and outward presentation. They know paedophilia is loathed in society and seen as the vilest of crimes. Some people may not be bothered if their neighbour was an ex-bank robber but few would feel comfortable with having a paedophile as a next-door neighbour. People cannot understand why God would forgive this sin. The acts of paedophile priests have distorted the life of the church and resulted in people viewing the church as evil. Priests I spoke to said that it is one thing people hating the church, but it is important that they do not end up hating God as a result of the actions of a percentage of paedophile priests. They must see the sins of the church but never forget the holiness of Jesus. The church remains the same. It's the human aspect of it that has become distorted and not the teachings of Jesus.

A lot of priests were convicted of sexual abuse with adolescents and young people. Did the maturity of these priests become arrested once they entered the seminary, owing to becoming 'starved' of intimacy from that moment onwards? Most priests I spoke with said they didn't know the reasons why some of their colleagues had sexually abused. Some shook their heads in dismay, and I believed were genuine in being as mesmerised as everybody else is as to why this darkness of the heart descended upon the church. A few of the priests offered opinions as to what may be the root cause. Fr Martin wondered if it was a case of pure paedophilia in the church or was it more about abusing power before adding the possibility of the abusing priests being arrested in emotional immaturity and development? Other priests, including Fr Charles, said he didn't know if it was a case of abusive authority, loneliness and isolation, or whether there was a deeper psychological malfunction — a distorted theology that led to these priests becoming sex abusers. Fr Daniel also mentioned loneliness as a strong possibility. He questions if years and years of prolonged and profound loneliness and emptiness left middle-aged priests crying out for affection and who unfortunately only found this in adolescents who they befriended through random circumstances. Daniel said he thought that much of the sexual abuse which took place was not pre-meditated but instead the result of a profound need for connection with another human being. Fr Gerry, on the other hand, asked if a repressed celibate priest who battled with his vows but did not want to 'break' them thought that sex with a child did not count as having sex. Gerry wondered if this distorted justification meant they allowed themselves to abuse children while retaining the idea that they were still faithful to their vows and to the church. He concluded though that clerical abuse also went on in the Anglican Church where there was as much a problem as in the Catholic Church despite it allowing married priests.

In Marie Keenan's book, *Child Sexual Abuse and the Catholic Church: Gender, Power, and Organizational Culture* (2011), five reasons were mentioned as to why paedophilia may manifest in priests, as follows:

▼ Insufficient consideration given to the theology of clerical sexuality, which prohibits male sexual expression by priests.
▼ A lifetime suppressing sexual desire has denied priests an important part of their humanity and needs scrutiny.
▼ An institutional life of celibacy has resulted in the prohibition of intimate relationships.
▼ Priests being expected to continually serve the needs of others often resulted in them neglecting their own needs, (including the sustaining of intimate friendships). In many instances this resulted in burnout.
▼ Formation training in seminaries totally lacks education on the development challenges that priests inevitability need to address, including sexuality, intimacy and touch.

Despite apologies and lots of rhetoric from the Vatican over the past decade or so, little has been done to increase confidence in the public that the Catholic Church will ever be open and transparent about its failings when it comes to protecting children from sexual abuse by priests. Having said that, Ireland has been fearless in exposing failures and recommending changes in the safeguarding of children through the Ferns, Ryan, Murphy and Cloyne reports. Every diocese and parish in Ireland now has safeguarding measures in place. Despite this progress, it must be acknowledged that the Vatican still lags behind in accountability and has thwarted transparency unless it has been obtained through legal powers.

▼ ▼ ▼

Some priests were so hurt by the shame they felt over the sex abuse scandals that it silenced their voices. They couldn't comprehend the trauma they were experiencing. When in public, many priests no longer wanted to be identified as priests and refrained from wearing their clerical collar. They have encountered abuse in the streets and endured name-calling including 'paedophile' by vengeful people who were hurt by the actions of abusing priests or used this merely as an excuse to be nasty and malicious. The Catholic Church is a huge organisation. Therefore it's hardly surprising that many priests were unaware of it happening. To put this into perspective, think of a family where abuse occurs when some members of that family are unaware. The same applies to the church with most priests remaining as oblivious as the public until the scandals unfolded one-by-one in the media.

Fr Anthony told me that he was in America in the early nineties when Brendan Smyth was arrested. He remembered feeling deep shock and found it hard to believe this had happened. He said many other priests like himself hadn't any idea that this kind of thing was occurring because it was never something they had any inkling of — not even a whisper — which Anthony knows some people will find difficult to believe but that is the truth. The media reporting on Smyth, even in the States, was extensive, making him grateful that he was away from Ireland at the time. The thought that people might believe that priests — any priest, including himself — could do something like this to a child was incredibly difficult to accept. He said he had never felt so much shame in his life, even though he hadn't personally done anything wrong.

Fr Oliver told me that ordinary priests had a terrible time because they didn't receive any support except from fellow priests. They just had to get on with it. There was little or no leadership or guidance on how to deal with the situation. It was simply unthinkable. Instead, priests were often asked to read cringe-worthy and embarrassing statements from bishops on the scandals and had no permission or authority to add their own personal thoughts and feelings. The media, at the same time, unleashed a tirade of criticism in their reporting. Feminists and journalists who were anti-clergy and who viewed the church as a patriarchal institution became relentless in their reporting. However, Oliver said that he knew of many priests who had received a tremendous amount of understanding and kindness from their parishioners — and who were genuinely sympathetic of the priest's position when scandal after scandal unfolded.

The fallout of the abuse scandals meant that many good priests were left to defend themselves without any help from the church. There was no counselling offered to priests, who in the main were left to cope with the crisis on their own. There was no properly developed support system that was designed to cope with something of this magnitude because the church had never before needed to handle a crisis so large. In some ways, perpetrators were better treated because, after they had served their prison sentences, they were given financial assistance by the church to help build new lives. Can you imagine how priests who were good and kind men and who brought compassion and commitment to their ministry must have felt? Here were men who were truly devoted to the church and almost overnight they started being treated with suspicion. Worse still, some were falsely accused of abuse, by people with thwarted motives, which had never actually taken place.

I asked several priests for their views on priests who had abused children. Fr William considers paedophile priests to be part of the deviance of life who are drawn towards Satan. He thinks they have a total lack of insight into the harm they have done and that it is like an addiction to them. He added that like addicts they are cunning and great liars and our minds can't keep up with them because they are ahead of us with their manipulation.

Fr Joseph told me the story of how he once knew a man who had been in prison for sexually abusing one of his children. The man couldn't understand why his wife wouldn't allow him home after his release. He couldn't grasp it, which rendered Joseph to almost asking him to realise what he had done. He cited this example as showing how blinkered paedophiles are — including paedophile priests who have little or no insight into the consequences of their actions and the impact it has had on their victims. Joseph concluded that their denial and lack of remorse borders on ruthlessness.

Fr Michael thinks the abusers were evil, and brought evil into the church. He said they had no love, no morals and were criminals. Michael added that they abused the life born in the womb; and not only the child but the victim's mother and father.

Fr Derek said the actions of paedophile priests immersed the church into a state of crime and sin. They insulted the faith they preached. Bishops who concealed these sinful actions destroyed any chance of reform, renewal or solidarity with the head and members of the mystical body of Christ. He added priests abused the Catholic Church and maybe even the children they baptised. They did it for their own sinful purposes. They knew it was a crime and would have a hole in their soul because of their criminal lust. Likewise, for bishops who aided and abetted the abusers. Derek said bishops are regarded as successors of the apostles, but the grace of their ordination was also destroyed. St Paul said that you must be obedient to the law but this means Civil Law first and not Canon Law.

Fr Frank said that every child who comes into the presence of a priest or bishop is received in the name of the Lord. An abusing cleric receives that child into his own presence and for his own sinful and criminal purposes. Frank also said the scandal of sexual abuse has changed people's opinion and that the institutional church is now looked upon as if it is engaged in an internal struggle between good and evil.

Fr Robert, an elderly priest I interviewed, said he knew two paedophile priests who had been removed from ministry but weren't too bothered by it. He said they told him it was nice to have sex with children. Robert said that priests like this were removed from their ministry, and removed from both a Christian understanding and Jesus. He felt it was all about control, but that God gives choices and freewill to every individual. Robert considered paedophile priests to be weak characters who indulge easily in self-pity — before adding that anybody can be a paedophile because God gave them that choice, just like he gave them the choice to be a murderer or not. Robert said those who abuse children know that what they are doing is wrong because it would be impossible for someone to train to be a priest and think otherwise.

▼ ▼ ▼

When I asked another priest, Fr Sean, if victims will ever forgive the church for what happened, his immediate response was 'I have'. He then went on to tell me his own personal story how as an eleven-year-old altar boy he was sexually abused by a priest. Sean said that most victims are offered compensation, apology and psychotherapy, but finding closure is the hardest. He decided to meet his abuser. He recalled how nervous he and his abuser were when they met. The abuser trembled when Sean asked him to hold his hands. The abuser said to Sean, 'But these are the hands that abused you,' to which Sean replied, 'That's why I asked for them.' Sean said that when they held hands he felt God's presence, which was like a healing balm. He pointed out that the purpose of these meetings is to benefit the victim not the perpetrator. It is a step towards lifting the trauma that can easily turn into lifelong damage and bitterness.

Many victims have complained about the meaningless apologies they received from the church. The public have listened to bishops — even the pope — speak out and make general apologies but the resonance of these has never felt enough to address the damage done. The words are always carefully chosen but they lack heart and sometimes integrity because they can sound prepared and scripted. Therefore, promises of no further cover-ups, together with assurances to do with revealing the truth about past secrecy and a zero tolerance approach towards any further abuse by clergy, are often viewed with skepticism, because they often sound rhetorical in tone and result in little or no change.

The truth is that victims are still frowned upon by the church and often, instead of being embraced, are ignored and pushed aside as unwanted entities because they act as reminders of the tremendous damage caused to the church by the abuse scandals. Even to this day, the church remains 'closed' and ill at ease with transparently disclosing information about abusing clerics. Past cover-ups remain secretively hidden, but for the church to properly heal it needs to reveal the truth that will uncover the remaining evil and criminality that has yet to be exposed. It needs to show itself capable of addressing this historical inability to self-reveal in order to move forward and regain some of its lost integrity. Can it ever rest knowing that victims were not treated with the respect and decency that Jesus would have afforded them?

Victims were often left in a vacuum of being unable to let go or forgive themselves, and questioning whether it was they or God who needed to forgive the abusers. They also often had to cope with being disowned by family and friends, when the abuse became openly known. Many victims of clerical sex abuse (as is the case with all sexual abuse) can suffer mental health issues in its aftermath. These issues range from self-harming, depression, suicidal ideation, shame and low self-esteem, anger, rage and grief. Some resort to alcohol and drugs to cope with the emotional turbulence. Others struggle with relationships. Trust becomes a crucial issue with an inability to form intimate sexual relationships.

A lot of the abuse that was uncovered, even at the height of the scandals, was historical rather than occurring at the time. This does not stop people wondering if abuse is still happening or questioning if it could happen again. This is impossible to say but certainly, the approach to leadership has changed. There is now better leadership nationally and at local level. The safeguarding of children is on the agenda to such a degree that it almost questions whether churches and priests are even safe for children. It's not uncommon for some priests to refuse to be alone with children and insist that another adult is present. Is this the correct message to be giving out to people and society? However, just because a system of protection is apparent, that does not mean that every bishop is adhering to it. The covering up of abuse became a way of life for many of them. The church was like the family — keep quiet, shut up and we will deal with it ourselves. But what was tolerable in the past is not tolerable now.

The response of the church is that clerical sex abuse should never have happened but there are safeguarding measures now in place. Intellectual and emotional maturity screening is carried out now before somebody joins a seminary. But what leads to a priest abusing children remains unanswered because the church has never explored it on a deep enough level to provide definite answers. Therefore, many questions have never been answered (nor asked) including whether paedophilia is linked to celibacy or if abusing priests know they were paedophiles when they joined the priesthood? Did they become priests with the deliberate intention of abusing children, or was it something which either revealed or generated itself while in the priesthood. Psychology is not an exact science, but questions must be asked. Silence does not produce answers, yet it seems that silence is the church's preferred choice when dealing with awkward and sensitive questions.

Some priests question if too much is being done in terms of safeguarding. Once an allegation is made, the priest must step aside (what happened to innocent until proven guilty?). It suffices to say that on paper a lot is being done but nothing explains why it happened. Are the safeguarding measures put in place meant to ensure it will never happen again? Or limit the opportunities to it occurring presently? Safeguarding measures are necessary but are they enough if the church remains in denial as a result of believing these alone will cure the malaise of paedophilia? They won't because, as you read earlier, paedophiles tend to be cunning and manipulative. Their deviation will remain in place and, ultimately, they will continue to find ways to abuse children.

My Christian understanding makes me believe that God loves everybody equally. It doesn't matter how rich or successful you are, God won't love you any more than he loves somebody who is homeless and begging on the streets. Most Christians will accept this concept but once you tell them that God loves the abused and the abuser equally, they tend to become less accepting. Admittedly, the abusers do terrible things to children. I have personally seen through my social work career the horrific long-term emotional damage that sexual abuse causes to individuals. In a metaphorical sense, something dies in the person's heart and shuts them down. People who abuse children, the impact they put on that child, goes on forever. But as Christians, should a morsel of empathy be given to priests who abused children? Could it be that some of them were sexually abused themselves when they were young? It is known that addictive paedophiles desire sex with young children and from the information known about clerical abuse cases, very few priests fell into this category. Instead, many were convicted of sexual liaisons with older children. Could this be a case of celibate, frustrated priests who were suffering from depression and loneliness and unable to control their sexual urges? Could it be that they were sexually and emotionally damaged? There are so many answers yet to transpire. We can now look back at Ireland over the last thirty years and view the full extent of the damage that clerical abuse has caused to the Irish Church. We also need to be aware that further crises may lie ahead, and consider whether a similar fate is going to befall the Catholic Church in countries like Poland, Africa, Philippines, South America and India, as well as others where Catholicism has a strong foothold. Time will tell.

Future New Church

And know that I am with you always;
yes, to the end of time.
(Jesus)
Matthew 28:20

Ireland, which was once deeply conservative, has seen the separation of church and state, leaving people to wonder what will happen to its future identity. Will it be okay to be Catholic in new liberal Ireland? Is the country going to learn from the mistakes of its past? Will it be able to heal divided hearts? Will priests, who often feel disillusioned and empty, find the willpower to help people develop a personal and profound relationship with Jesus? One way or another people will continue to seek God and spirituality because there is an innate human curiosity towards the divine, which will create new spiritual awareness either in the post-Catholic Irish Church or completely outside of it. Time is of the essence and time appears to be running out for the church in its current format.

Catholicism in Ireland up to and including the 1970s was about praying and obeying. It was a cultural norm — a blind faith and authority led. Some say it came with a pathology that was a seductive sickness because of its rule-based hierarchical structure that imposed teachings of fear. After the clerical sex abuse scandals, people began to hate the church and reject its teachings. People began to resent it for what it represented. The last twenty years has seen the church in a crisis — maybe even more than a crisis. Many people feel that unless radical action is taken, the situation won't be rectified. Others feel that it is too late to do anything about it because although some hostility towards the church is waning, it is replaced with a new phase of apathy. It is seen by the general public as indifferent and irrelevant in a fast-moving world. Basically, it is felt that most people no longer care about the church or its future. Priests are aware of how people feel and there is much anger that matters have come to this. There are priests who admit the church is dysfunctional and in denial of its crisis even though the evidence is staring such priests in the face. But they don't want to wake up to reality. Other clergy feel that there are no 'prophets' in the church hierarchy of bishops and senior clerics who, in the main, carry out their ministry with no vision or motivation for reform (and who hold little accountability). The current senior figures consist of insiders who are either career priests or bishops. They have little to offer regarding renewal and reform of the church.

Priests in general predict that the Irish Catholic Church of the future will be a smaller institution than present. To prevent the current institution from shrinking any further and dying, the church will need to bring in more lay people and train them to use their gifts and creativity. Does a theology of kindness and more open-mindedness in line with modern day Ireland need to take root? Will the church need to act out of love and social justice for people to start believing in it again?

Regarding the future of the church, a priest I spoke to called Fr Anthony said that reform will not be achieved within its current structure. Catholicism for many has become a civil religion. It has lost its true meaning — lost its religious dimension. For some clergy the abortion referendum showed apostasy towards the church because it showed that there were people who attended Mass who did not believe in its teachings. Anthony said priests are beginning to wonder if anybody is still interested in their preaching — and so are feeling a need to pull back. Anthony feels the time will come when priests become so demoralised they will be unable to continue in their ministry. He feels the clergy will need to rebuild the religion from the ground up. It will and must return to be a more evangelical type of religion that will enable people to develop a spiritualism which will nurture them. This is where the emphasis needs to be. The church needs to plot its way forward. Only then, Anthony feels, will people start to view it as a committed church which is assuming responsibility.

Faith in Christianity appears to be vanishing in Ireland because of the betrayal of trust, and has got to the point where communication between the church and laity is difficult at best — and in some cases impossible. In its present structure, compassion and forgiveness for it are proving difficult. New beginnings need to take root. One of the ways forward and which is being encouraged by the pope is the introduction of a synodal church structure. This would be a church that holds everybody, including the clergy, as people of God. A church where everybody is made to feel they belong, that they are good enough and entitled to bring something of use to the continuation and running of the church. This would be a church where clergy and laity would work alongside each other in dialogical ways to ensure that every baptised Catholic would have their voice listened to. The local people in each community would get the chance to express their views as to what they want to see happen. These days, people are very educated and make up their own minds quickly. The synodal church would combine theology and philosophy. It would be about learning to love one another by acknowledging the true meaning of Jesus. It would become a faith with the ability to heal and would bring compassion back to its central core. It would prioritise the poor and the marginalised. It would become much more concerned about the environment and climate change.

Priests are not against this idea of synod gatherings in principle, but in most cases getting the idea off the ground and put into action is still at an embryonic stage. Fr Leo felt that people need to come together to be the new voice of the church and to take part in the decision- making and thought processes. This will include the public exchange of opinions at synod gatherings. This will entail moving away from purely relying on Roman governance to becoming the church of the people, where everybody is involved — while not damaging the universal communion of Catholicism. Fr Martin said that a synod church would allow room for the interpretation of the gospels. It might even create a pathway that will allow theological diversity in key topics like homosexuality, celibacy and ordination of female priests. The big question, though, is whether it will create a battle between liberal and conservatives who often have strong opposing views on these topics.

For real change to take root, future clergy will need to learn from the mistakes of the past and act differently from their predecessors if a new, healthy church is to emerge. People of all ages need to have a church where they are invited to get to the heart of what life is all about and to taste the mystery of God (including its love and wonder). The initial aim of the 'new' church must be to ensure there is something worthwhile on offer, so as to entice people back.

Therefore, the church as we know it must be utterly different from the past. There needs to be an agenda that would allow new ideas to be discussed, including:

- ▼ An ethos of power and control to be handed back to the people.
- ▼ More volunteers to be recruited.
- ▼ Priests and bishops to be community elected.
- ▼ Compulsory celibacy to be discussed.
- ▼ Women deacons to be allowed.
- ▼ Less emphasis on Canon Law (which is manmade rather than divine revelation).

▼ ▼ ▼

The current crisis should be seen as an opportunity because it is going to bring about true and lasting change. The new church will be a combined cooperation of the clergy and laity which will have the potential to bring fresh insights and perspectives. At present, while people may have given up on the church, they have not given up on life. People need to have a faith and spirituality in their lives because sooner or later life will confront every person alive where they are unable to back away or bury it. Ultimately, people have always had a yearning to have questions answered about the purpose and meaning of life. Enticing young people and indeed adults back to the church will be a challenge. Currently there is little to offer, although this could change over time if the church proves it wants to reform and is capable once more to be at the heart of its communities and the people it serves.

Despite the many changes Ireland has seen since in recent decades, the church remains steadfast in its teachings which it feels should not be altered. However, several of the priests I spoke to admitted that the Irish Church and its current practices must change, or risk even further decline. Fr Paul said the Catholic Church is still a church of mercy because Jesus preached with compassion. However, that does not mean that change and reform must take place at any cost. Some warn of not falling into the trap of thinking that if the church wants to be modern, they will have to do XYZ.

Another priest, Fr Jack, said some priests feel the church does not court popularity and that its message is to simply preach — which people are then free to accept or reject. An example of this was the abortion referendum. This caused great sadness to those who wanted children but were unable to conceive — or those who had miscarriages in the past. Jack said it was demoralising to realise that so many innocent lives are lost as a result of the outcome of the referendum. Jack said the revolt was an indication of the culture that we live in, forming part of 'me and my rights', whereby nobody seems capable of taking advice from anybody else these days — but instead prefer to do their own thing.

In recent years, a new wave of priests has started coming to Ireland from Africa, India, Poland and Slovakia. They are not the answer to the shortage of priests in Ireland. It is noticed, even within citizen clergy, that priests from abroad come with a frightening harshness and lack of compassion — and too, it is felt that they patronise Irish people. Older bishops may say that Ireland gave our priests to Africa in the last century and that it's only right they come to us now in return. They fail to appreciate the difference between the third world back then that had never heard of the gospels and the first world country of Ireland which is now post-Catholic. These priests are not the answer because their rigid theology is simply not going to work in the Ireland of today.

Another priest, Fr Kieran, also didn't hold much hope or regard towards African priests becoming part of Irish ministry in larger numbers, as he feels they act in a superior manner towards ordinary people. Some, he claimed, show disrespect towards women, and others run closed parish councils and liturgy groups because they view females in a patriarchal way and therefore as inferior to the word of a priest. This is the way they were trained as priests in Africa to act as a law above everybody else. Kieran also referred to the problems with communication owing to heavily accentuated accents. Kieran wasn't being racist or discriminatory, rather his views were based on his own experiences and those of some colleagues. Kieran also believes that the church in Africa is on the periphery of sexual abuse cases coming to light involving priests and women. While remarking upon Kieran's comments to an English friend who had lived in Africa for several years, I was told that it was the custom in Africa for Catholic priests in a village to have a 'wife' in the sense that a woman was reserved for him to visit for sexual purposes. It was deemed the norm to have this sense of entitlement to have sexual relationships with women. It would seem celibacy in Africa leaves a lot to be desired.

▼ ▼ ▼

Young people in Ireland don't seem to have the reservations of their parents' or grandparents' generation. Although most of the young are not actively involved in the church (and thus attending Mass and receiving the sacraments don't feature largely on their horizons), they nevertheless have an openness which could potentially blossom into something dynamic and vibrant — provided they are listened to and respected. Their souls are like everybody else's on the planet — they need nourishment. It is said if the soul does not get nourishment from religion or spirituality, it will look elsewhere for solace. Thomas Moore, the eighteenth century Irish poet once wrote: 'The great malady implicated in all our troubles and affecting us individually and socially is "loss of soul". When soul is neglected, it doesn't just go away; it appears symptomatically in obsession, addiction, violence and loss of meaning. Although it is a global trend and not just something occurring in Ireland, the fact that young Irish people have, in the main, turned their backs on the church and Mass doesn't make it any less saddening. And yet they haven't turned their backs on God, prayer and a quest to find a deeper meaning and purpose in their lives. It's not an easy time for priests to be expected to entice young people back to religion. Priests understand young people struggle to accept church teachings on controversial issues such as contraception, abortion, homosexuality, cohabitation and marriage. Many priests, irrespective of their age, are frightened of young people making false allegations against them despite the safeguarding measures in place. Many priests feel uncomfortable around young people and vice versa. But this is not the same throughout all priesthood, or from diocese to diocese, or parish to parish. For example, you might find a parish in Co. Limerick with a middle-aged priest who is actively participating in youth ministry projects, whereas, a parish perhaps in Co. Roscommon might have an elderly priest without the interest or vitality necessary to engage with young people. However, youth ministry exists and is developed either by individual priests or through religious orders like Franciscan priests and Dominican nuns. Collectively, the numbers are still relatively low but nevertheless this does not diminish the good work youth ministries do for young people. A main part of youth ministry is prayer groups as these have proved popular for some young people to think and reflect on life, exam stress and future education and employment opportunities. Volunteering is also part of youth ministry groups, where, for example, a group of secondary school students help with taking elderly parishioners to Lourdes. As well, leadership groups, where training is provided on what it means to be part of a community, are combined with a little religion, including prayers and meditation. It has been found that these groups teach good teamwork skills which enable young people to develop self-confidence and a sense of belonging. Some young people have completed school projects after their training on topics like bullying prevention and environment issues and have helped others as a result of the skills learned through the training.

Clergy and lay people behind youth ministry programmes have accepted that attending Mass is not the only way to God for young people. They know that Mass no longer speaks to young people and that there is very little to hold them within the current remit of the church. The church itself must accept that it is not raising a generation of Mass goers and must become creative in how it get its message across to young people — and that the main way of doing so is through schools, colleges and educational institutions. It is here where many young people experience their only contact with the church and, in some ways, such 'light touch religion' becomes an alternative to becoming more involved with the church. The church is also becoming aware of the power of social media and is valuing Facebook, Twitter and Instagram as a means of attracting young followers. In doing so, the church is aware that it has a duty to tap into what young people are seeking. It knows that deep down there is a craving for spiritual nourishment and the only way the church can appeal to the young is to make them feel welcomed by being honest, transparent, inviting, accessible and joyful. Young people in Ireland, at least for the foreseeable future, won't return to an institutionally rigid church and therefore a more rational, all-inclusive approach needs to be on offer, which welcomes without judging individuals for not following the perceived (historical) standards. One priest, Fr Richard, who I spoke to about youth ministry, told me that despite all that has happened to the Irish Church, he still has great hope in young Irish people. He said the country is blessed in having so many young people with good hearts. Richard said he has seen their willingness to engage in various programmes, along with their great sense of social justice, fun and joy.

Fr Pat, who also works in youth ministry, accepts that the church has a lot to learn from young people and appreciates the current difficult relationship that many young people have with the traditional church. Pat admits that transcending the institutional structure of the church, so as to assist finding God, spirituality and peace, has worked for many young people via various events and workshops which have taken place under the umbrella of the youth ministry. From feedback from those who had completed various programmes, it is clear that many have been able to find faith in a different context to that provided by an 'official' church building. Others felt that participating in workshops acted as a wonderful reminder to look for God in everybody. It also helped them to think more about other people's circumstances rather than just their own. Others said that they were able to focus on building a relationship with God as a result of being able to talk freely with other young people without the fear of being ridiculed for having a faith/religion. They felt a relaxed approach in workshops which involved laughter, singing, dancing and storytelling, which made events more interesting and uplifting.

When I was young, benediction used to bore me intensely and I usually couldn't wait for it to end. Perhaps its purpose wasn't explained properly or maybe priests took it for granted that people understood and valued its purpose. To my surprise, I notice that Eucharist adoration (i.e. benediction) is one of the three core activities of Youth 2000, an international youth movement set up under Pope John Paul II during his pontificate. Youth 2000 was first set up in Ireland in 1993 and can be found in every province with over 30 groups currently in existence across Ireland. The second core component is devotion to Our Lady and reciting the rosary and the third is fidelity and faithfulness to the teachings of the Catholic Church. Membership is open to those aged 16–35 and tends to be comprised of those from conservative middle-class backgrounds, although anybody from any socio-economic background or level of belief is welcome to join. Although individual groups are small, annual retreats see young people come together from all over the country and provide a positive vibe where young people join in prayer. This helps form friendships with like-minded people, be it at a summer gathering or coming together to celebrate World Youth Day. In addition to annual national gatherings, prayer groups exist in local areas where young people regularly meet for prayer, silence, music, reflection or to read scripture.

Youth 2000 is often seen as a way of sharing the Catholic faith among young people — by young people. Members are generally regarded as being more religious than young people involved in other youth ministry-associated groups. Many regularly attend mass. Some will train to be Eucharistic ministers. Recent vocations to the priesthood have come from some members of this youth group.

Although small in numbers and fairly randomly dispersed throughout the country, youth groups like those just mentioned are inroads to rebuilding a new church and/or forums for arriving at new ways to think about faith, God and life. It is felt they are needed to stem the pervasive conditions of society, whereby young people often don't have the ability to think for themselves. Fr Eamon told me a story about a young secondary school student who was part of his local youth ministry group who wrote disparaging comments about the Catholic Church on Facebook at the time of the abortion referendum. Eamon said he wished he hadn't read them because they caused him upset. He said he had known the young person all his life and knew the boy had never had a bad experience of the church, yet he wrote things about the church that couldn't conceivably be based on his own experiences. All too often, a culture has been devised (irrespective of whether somebody has had negative experiences) that allows them to feel they have the right to be anti-establishment in order to look favourable among their peers. It was this culture that made it seem okay for a young person to say that people should vote 'yes' in the abortion referendum to get back at the church without understanding or articulating the grievance they demonstrate towards the church.

▼ ▼ ▼

Some priests claim that the Catholic Church hasn't changed. They say the church is still the same but attitudes towards it have changed, including those of some clergy. The reality is, however, that the aging clergy means some priests are looking after several parishes and this is unsustainable. The decline in church attendances is also at crisis point. In Irish cities, it is estimated that only 25 percent of people attend Mass regularly but the numbers in rural parishes are a little higher (a third). Nationally, it is believed that only two-thirds of Irish Catholics attend services at least once a month. Of this figure, under a quarter of young Irish Catholics (those aged between 16 and 29) are thought to go to Mass every week. Many dioceses have seen few vocations in over a decade. The possibility of church closures is real and the only way to prevent this happening is for more lay people to become directly responsible for their churches. In the absence of priests, lay services will need to take place, with only occasionally a priest saying Mass. It is envisaged that probably only one church per parish will be fully functioning. Older people currently provide much of the financial support to the church which upon their passing will be lost. Middle-aged people generally display an indifference to the church irrespective of whether they attend Mass. For others, perhaps the hardest thing to do is to walk humbly with God especially after the affluence and greed of the Celtic Tiger boom years — a time when people stopped attending Mass. This combined with the aftermath of the clerical sex abuse scandals saw faith for many coming to a halt. Some do return from time to time. Funerals are still very important in Ireland. People attend funerals and make connections to the point they start coming back to Mass. Weddings, baptisms, first Holy Communion and confirmations also remind attendees of their religion. Perhaps these events provide an opportunity for people to reflect on their lives and God, albeit for the briefest of moments. Others see their parents dying and their faith is restored around that experience. Of course, others will never return though because God no longer comes into their way of thinking.

Religion in Ireland in the past was very cultural and was generally what people did. But time has moved on. The church saw the collapse of an 'ideal' by the idealists (clergy) after they did not live up to their preaching. The people believed the church to be a naturally trusted ideal with every fibre. The church was everything. The church got everything, but the church lost touch with working-class areas in cities and failed to relate their liturgy to the poor. But in order to move forward we must recognise that things of the past are a spent force. The 'new' church will have to be in touch with people and consider what is happening in people's lives. It will have to converse in a language that is understood by ordinary people.

It will need to understand that the most immoral behaviour in society today belongs to the financial and political powers of the world where malice, greed and hate are commonplace. Sexual sins are no longer considered the most important. The priests of the future must not be accorded the opportunity to live life in a bubble or an ivory tower. They must live in their own time and have an unwavering commitment to their ministry. What they preach must be relevant, rational and reasonable; it must bridge the gap between what is happening in the world today and the teachings of Jesus. The new church must not be an authoritarian church. It must converse in a meaningful way to people and their lives but equally not be afraid to challenge negativity and harm.

Another priest, Fr Eddie, said that for some people the church remains a place of belonging in their community. It holds a caring presence even for those who don't come frequently, but may instead visit occasionally to say a prayer or light a candle. It continues to be a place of welcome, a place of stability, a haven of peace during the troubles and struggles of life, especially during times of bereavement. Even if change remains slow and unyielding, it is nevertheless envisaged that in ten years' time, many people in Ireland will still come to pray and receive the sacraments.

A further priest, Fr Martin, said the gospels are the template for Christian living because Jesus clearly set out in the beatitudes how merciful, kind and loving God is to every human being on the planet. The old church did not put love first because it readily condemned. The new church, in order to grow, needs to love first and then ask questions. Martin said priests are as guilty as anybody else for failing to remember this principle and all too often have got embroiled themselves in envy, suspicion and hate of others. Priests have a ringside view of the events that shape people's lives. They help make memories at baptisms, weddings and funerals. Martin concluded that priests must not be complacent or arrogant or adopt a 'holier than thou' stance towards others. They must remember that they too have feet of clay.

▼▼▼

Seminaries, like priests, have dwindled in existence with only three seminaries left for the training of Irish priests. The largest is St Patrick's in Maynooth, founded in 1795 and designed to house 500 trainees. It was once the largest seminary in the world. It currently houses less than 25 seminarians, the youngest is aged 18 and the oldest 55. The average age of men joining the priesthood in Ireland is currently between 25–30 years of age. This is its lowest ever figure, with just a handful of men preparing to cater for the 3.7 million Irish people who consider themselves Catholic or at least Catholic by birth. The numbers of seminarians began to slowly decline in the '80s, although current figures are remarkably low in comparison to those of 10–15 years ago which saw numbers dropping from 120 down to 80. Future projection could see an increase in numbers in the coming years but only by small fractions. The number of priests in Ireland has fallen to just over 3,900 but their age is the bigger problem. Some priests view the current situation as grave and readily point out that if you have no priest, then you have no Mass, and if you have no Mass, then you have no church. There are over 200 parishes in Dublin alone with fewer than 400 priests to run these. St Patrick's is not giving up looking for new vocations to the priesthood but are seeking emotionally mature candidates who can sustain the harsh societal negativity towards the church while having the willpower to devote their lives to ministry and the reforms needed for the Irish church to survive. Some accusations though have been directed towards newly ordained priests from Maynooth stating that some are very traditional in their attitudes. Some are said to lean towards Latin Mass and traditional dress, although these are low in number.

The second seminary with close links to St Patrick's seminary is the Pontifical Irish College in Rome, which has around a dozen seminarians. Once ordained these priests will be assigned back to their diocese of origin. Rumours surround the possibility of whether St Patrick's seminary or the Pontifical Irish College will amalgamate at some point in the future if the number of seminarians remains low. The Pontifical Irish College wins praise for having a broader curriculum than St Patrick's where it is said that greater focus is placed on affection, human sexuality and the psychological and emotional needs of priests in its formation programme.

The third seminary is a new Irish missionary seminary; the Redemptoris Mater Seminary in Dundalk was formed in 2012. This is a Catholic evangelical movement called 'Neocatechumenal Way' which is endorsed by the Vatican. It currently has over twenty seminarians who come from a range of European countries including Ireland. The seminarians receive their formation in Dundalk but travel to St Patrick's in Maynooth for their philosophical and theological studies. These priests will be exclusively ordained as priests of the Archdiocese of Armagh, although some may be sent abroad to do missionary work.

During my visit to St Patrick's seminary I was told that priests are under no illusion that they are often viewed as eccentric and sometimes out of touch, although they refute these claims. They are aware that society views priests unfavourably owing to their vows of celibacy, and fail to consider that priests experience a different kind of affection in their lives. With regards to taking vows of celibacy they feel that every priest is in a committed relationship with the church and as a result their celibacy is part of how they serve God. Celibacy is still viewed in its original context of a priest being forbidden to have sex with a woman.

Lessons have been learnt from the past and it is privately acknowledged (even if not publicly) that up until recently, priests often graduated from their seminary training unprepared for life and, sometimes, with damaged and dysfunctional personalities. These days, men interested in the priesthood are asked to reflect on their decision to become a priest for at least two years before joining the seminary to ensure they have the correct motivation and understanding of the life that lies ahead of them. There is also a new formation programme in place aimed at assisting each seminarian to get to know themselves better. It consists of four dimensions: human, spiritual, intellectual and pastoral. These pillars are designed to ensure priests leave the seminary with balanced and healthy minds — and that they truly know themselves. The curriculum also teaches them to relate to their 'self' and others in the best possible way. This includes discussing sexuality, sexual orientation and desire. Each seminarian has a private mentor, with whom they meet regularly for private discussion and reflection. This is designed to help them to get to really know themselves as a person. It is here where unhealthy attitudes towards pornography and indeed children may be unearthed and acted upon.

The current reaction to homosexuality at St Patrick's is cautious and neutral in the sense that it is neither condoned nor accepted. But, ultimately, I formed the impression that they would be better pleased if they didn't have to discuss the issue. The discussion of the ordination of women priests is also firmly off limits at St Patrick's, in line with Vatican governance about the issue. It is also not a subject high on the agenda for debate in the future. Though it is recognised that the church has not always been kind to women and should avail of the gifts of women, its stance remains in line with Pope Francis who has long insisted that women cannot be priests because Jesus was a man. However, in other discussions Francis has emphasised that women, not men, were chosen by God to be the first witnesses of the resurrection. Criticisms from priests directed at St Patrick's include that it remains an all-male institution, with little or no female influence upon seminarians, even if just to prepare them to work alongside women in the future church.

Forward thinking is part of critical reforms being set out by St Patrick's which includes a vision for the church based on projected low numbers. It is said that the new Irish Church will produce more intentional Catholics and restore the ability to feel proud of being a Catholic. The future role of the priest remains the same — to preach the gospel and administer the sacraments. Admittedly, priesthood is no longer seen as an attractive life option with parents often dissuading their sons from joining. Even some priests themselves refrain from encouraging young men to join because they too have grown tired of its uncertainty.

That said, some important and interesting developments are being created in the Irish church. One of the church's answers to the lack of new men joining the priesthood and its existing aging priests was its attempt to introduce more deacons. However, again, only males can be deacons. They can be married when they join but if their wife dies they are not allowed to remarry. Some say their role has little substance — they can minister over baptisms, weddings and funerals but are not allowed to say Mass or hear confessions. There are currently only a few dozen in the country, mainly in larger cities. Training to be a deacon takes four years and is undertaken through St Patrick's seminary, culminating in a Diploma in Diaconal Studies.

A more pragmatic move for the future of the Irish Church is the proposed introduction of pastoral assistants (male and female) into the church. The introduction of this role is to recognise that all Catholics are equal, but accounts for everybody having different roles and gifts to bring into the church. It is in line with the vision of the Second Vatican Council which stipulated that every baptised Catholic has a gift to share. However, if pastoral assistants are to become a reality, a greater involvement from lay people in church matters will be required. In general, the introduction of pastoral assistants has been sidelined or poorly acted upon by various popes since it was first mentioned in the Second Vatican Council reforms in the 1960s. The proposal is that non-ordained members will carry out duties like deacons, but will have more involvement in helping parents prepare their children for baptism, and carry out marriage preparations groups and catechism groups (for all ages). Much of the training to become pastoral assistants would be done through St Patrick's. It is hoped this new role will be introduced into every diocese and parish in Ireland over the next few years.

▼ ▼ ▼

One priest, Fr Simon, remarked to me that these days whenever he meets with colleagues, conversation is invariably about retirement, pensions, old age and sickness. It is all about looking inwards. He added that it is hard to see anything in the church blossoming when there is no vitality. Young people have no desire to engage, although pockets of youth ministry across the country provide some spiritual nourishment as previously mentioned.

Again with young people, discrepancies in accounts suggest on one hand that young people do not have the reservations about the church that belongs to their parents' and grandparents' generations but on the other hand young people can say disparaging things that don't relate to their own personal experiences and are based on hearsay. But whatever account is true or not, the unmistakeable fact staring everyone in the face is an aging clergy and smaller and smaller congregations with each passing year. This does not place the church in a position to offer hope of a revival. The Irish Church is currently well and truly in liquidation. It will continue to shrink and shrink, and then what? Certainly priesthood needs re-defining but do answers lie in removing compulsory celibacy and allowing priests to marry? Or would allowing the ordination of women bring revival despite the Vatican's strict veto of these measures? Perhaps neither of these would make any difference now, given it might be that the decline will not be able to be halted — or even would make little difference to the rebuilding of the damaged empire that was once the Irish Church. Nevertheless, some attempts at reform exist including the following;

We are Church Ireland (which is part of *We Are Church International*) was set up in Ireland in 2012, in the hope of introducing a democratic structure into the church, based on consensus and the wishes and feelings of most people. It is a forum for discussion and reform and believes that people should be heard. This is moving away from the notion that the clergy know everything and that the laity is forbidden to discuss anything, because discussion leads to action and action leads to change.

There are five aims of *We Are Church Ireland:*

- ▼ Decision making actively shared by all.
- ▼ Full participation of women in all ministries.
- ▼ Primacy of conscience.
- ▼ Remove obligation of clerical celibacy.
- ▼ An inclusive church welcoming to all.

In many ways, the ideology of *We are Church Ireland* is like the concept of the synodal church in the sense that it involves the voices of everybody. As well as being liberal, it advocates change in key areas, including the lifting of celibacy and the ordination of women. There are two things that are important to know about *We Are Church Ireland:* firstly, every member was born a Catholic and most still attend weekly Mass, and secondly, members are liberal Catholics who are pressing for change in the Catholic Church to ensure it becomes more diverse and inclusive. It also advocates for the inclusivity of the LGBT community where priests could be open about their sexual orientation and be able to marry their same sex partners.

We are Church Ireland is mindful of the future changes that will see few active parishes because of priest shortage and resources. However, it is envisaged that instead of Mass, there will be lay services where members of the laity carry out readings from the gospels and engage in spiritual discussion. Occasionally, a priest will come to say Mass or, alternatively, parishioners will travel to churches on a rota basis wherever a Mass is taking place.

We are Church Ireland currently hold monthly meetings in Dublin where members, including women who have vocations and former priests who left to get married, meet for impromptu services consisting of them celebrating their own form of the Eucharist where they hold out their hands in celebration of the divine. They are aware that this puts them on the outside of the church but groups like this are expected to grow in the coming years with many people already showing high interest in the current framework. Groups like this are returning to grassroots level where it is hoped the church will eventually play catch up after they start listening to people.

The Roncalli movement is another reform initiative in formation in Dublin. A handful of priests are aspiring to get it up and running in some Dublin parishes as a trial but have long-term ambitions to see it become rooted in other dioceses across the country. Roncalli was the surname of Pope John XXIII who became a surprise pope. When he was appointed, his papacy was expected to be brief owing to his poor health. He was seen as a stop-gap, an elderly pontiff that wouldn't cause too much upheaval in the church but instead he revolutionised the church during his five-year reign until his death of pancreatic cancer in 1963, more than any other pope in the last few centuries. Roncalli refused to be kowtowed to the curia and instead showed his strength and clear sense of vision in developing an inclusive church that would sustain change, welcome more women into roles within the church, as well bringing about church unity. He had a great sense of humour and upon his appointment as pope when asked by a reporter how many priests worked in the Vatican, he promptly replied "about a third of them".

This new movement, primarily formed by Fr Joe MacDonald (author of *Why the Irish Church Deserves to Die*), aims to implement his vision set out in the second Vatican Council with its core aims to be an association of reform and renewal in the Irish Church. It hopes to implement the changes that never became actualised by successive popes since Roncalli. This new movement in Ireland, which has the blessings of the Irish clerical hierarchy, will aim to deliver more radical changes, including more of the feminine into the church and re-introducing people to the teachings of Jesus. It will enshrine all of the teachings of the Catholic Church but will not be a splinter group. The vision is for a community base — for example, maybe four to five members of the group, including a priest, will live together –with the possibility that a female administrator will be in charge of the parish as opposed to a priest. The founders of this movement are fully aware that the Irish Church of the future will be a smaller church, but they hope to become a bastion of prayer and study and revitalise Catholicism with passion and commitment and be a place of welcome to everybody including the LGBT community.

▼ ▼ ▼

Many people who attended Mass in the past switched off when the gospel was preached because in old style Catholicism there was never any encouragement to read or learn about the teachings of Jesus. Fr Daniel told me that even to this day some priests preach about God as the God of the laws as opposed to the God of compassion. Failure to impart how much God loves mankind and how much we ought to love God as opposed to fearing him remains in place for some clergy. It's what they are used to and while they may no longer preach harsh sermons, there will be aspects of pious spirituality in their preaching which advises how people should live if they expect to get to heaven. Daniel said there is no emphasis on social justice, which ignores the core messages of the gospels. But, because of focusing so heavily on the afterlife, priests have often neglected, and at times completely ignored, the real-life, daily sufferings of the poor. This is in total contradiction to the message of Jesus and the gospels, particularly Mark's Gospel (25:36) *I was naked and you clothed me; I was sick and you took care of me; I was in prison and you visited me.* The four gospels — Matthew, Luke, Mark and John — are all different accounts into the life and teachings of Jesus. But what is consistent in all the gospels is the love and compassion Jesus had for everybody and his constant quest for truth-telling, self-sacrifice and fairness in society. He was never preoccupied with sex and sexuality or the continuous morality teachings of how to live life to get to heaven that blighted the Irish Church for so long. The church of the future must learn from past mistakes if it is to reveal Jesus' tenderness which it previously denied itself and its people for such a long time.

The future of the church in Ireland is largely seen as one that will be lay led, but also one which will be restored in health and enthusiasm. In among the laity will be priests, albeit fewer in number but better trained and better equipped to deal with societal changes and attitudes. The voice of the church will make itself heard in its belief that it has something valuable to offer to the good of humanity, which is something that perhaps a lot of priests have lost sight of in recent decades while coping with the abuse scandals and the melting of public support and goodwill towards the church. The new church will have vision and hope where Irish Catholics can walk into the future less concerned about self-reverence but more concerned in believing that they are on a journey together. It is felt that the pain and destruction revealed over the past thirty years has been a good thing. It is a cleansing of the bad and evil, making way for growth, renewal and ultimately the rebirth of something better.

The words of the Eucharistic prayer at a Catholic funeral Mass spring to mind, *Remember, Lord, those who have died and have gone before us marked with the sign of faith*. I would hope that among the plethora of changes that will occur over the next decade or two as the old church withers away and a reformed church takes its place is that babies still get baptised because deep down I still fundamentally believe that Catholicism is a good religion and can be great again one day in Ireland. Baptism is a seed that can be left to grow irrespective of whether somebody practises their faith, but can anybody ever really go through life without the need to call upon God for help at some point or other? As you will have read in this book and perhaps experienced in your own life, the old church let many people down. I think the time will come to forgive the church for what it did and move on with life. Now would seem a good time to start.

That's not to say that before reform and renewal occurs that further changes in the church won't bring sadness and fear for some people. Church closures are expected within the next ten years. I visited one in Dublin which was nearing its end. It wasn't an old church, having only been built in 1967, but its roof required extensive repairs. Sadly, fundraising attempts failed to raise anywhere near the amount of money required to carry out the essential maintenance. Its closure caused upset to its parishioners — the remaining faithful who attended Mass there every Sunday. For many, it will have been like bidding farewell to an old friend who weathered the ups and downs of life alongside them for many years. I felt a feeling of sadness in the place during my visit, as my psyche took in its demise. Undoubtedly more of this type of sadness will occur before a new dawn arises with new beginnings, new opportunities and the start of a new and better Irish Church.

I mentioned earlier in the book that I am a lapsed Catholic who attends church services a few times a year. Would I go back on a regular basis? As I previously explained, it's where I feel most at home, having being raised in the faith. With regards to returning on a frequent basis, I am open to persuasion and will eagerly watch the reforms and renewals that take place in the coming years. Will hypocrisy still continue to linger over sexuality or the reluctance of the church to admit that a great many Catholic priests are gay? Frankly, I don't care if a priest is straight or gay provided he is a good man with a good heart. I don't have strong opinions against women becoming ordained. I suspect paedophile priests may still seek to abuse children despite the new stringent safeguarding which has been put in place. The pathology behind such drives and behaviour needs uprooting and questioning in terms of whether compulsory celibacy, coupled with an inability to cope with a life without sex, are responsible key factors.

Attending confession is out for me as I fail to see its relevance. I believe people are perfectly capable of asking God directly for forgiveness. On a separate note, I don't think God is the least bit bothered what type of sex people have. Furthermore, I also don't believe a person's soul is affected one iota if they don't practise their religion. I believe God sees every soul and knows exactly what type of life each person leads. Church attendance and adherence to a faith are not compulsory requirements to leading a good life. A friend told me how much her elderly mother feared death and hell before she died. So why should this woman who had lived a simple, hard-working life, who raised a family and never did anything seriously wrong in her life believe that God would punish her mercilessly upon death. But that is what this lady expected after being indoctrinated by the church in the pray and obey bygone days. I believe in the God of love and compassion and not the vengeful God of law and obedience that was consistently instilled into many people from childhood.

We must never return to such old ways of the church again. The parents and grandparents of those belonging to my generation will now mainly have passed away. Didn't we bury our dead well? Many will have been like my friend's mother who feared death. I believe most of these people will have been extremely good people and that God's love for them is endless. I also believe that many a good priest and nun, of which there will have been ample throughout the ages, will equally join in God's eternal love. What has happened to the Irish Church has happened and cannot be undone. There is no turning back. Rather, we should look towards the future, with enthusiasm and belief that the Irish Church can rebirth itself into something new and profoundly magnificent. I believe the best is yet to come and I am grateful that I am still young enough to see it become a reality one day.

ACKNOWLEDGEMENTS

I discovered from an early stage that finding priests willing to participate in interviews for my book wasn't an easy task. The mere mention of the words 'homosexual' and 'paedophile' did little to encourage them to come forward and voice their opinions. However, thirty priests did put their heads above the parapet and allowed their voices to be heard. I offer all of them my sincere thanks and appreciation. While I did not always entirely agree with some of their views, I acknowledge their courage in being able to say how they felt on the various topics which are often contentious for priests to discuss.

I would like to thank Fr. Tomás Surlis (Pro-Rector of the Seminary at Saint Patrick's College, Maynooth), Fr. Peter McVerry (Peter McVerry Trust) and Colm Holmes (We are Church Ireland) for their time and assistance.

I would also like to offer my gratitude to Fr. Bernárd Lynch for his wisdom and encouragement and to thank him for writing the foreword to the book. I would also like to extend thanks to Fr. Joe McDonald for reading the manuscript and writing such a lovely reflection afterwards. Joe's good sense of humour during interviews was also something I won't forget.

I would also like to extend thanks to all my wonderful friends in Donegal who kindly and freely contributed to the chapter 'Ireland Today'.

Thanks also to my editorial team — Michelle Emerson and Angela Stokes for their help and assistance. Finally, special recognition and appreciation goes to Simona Summers at *The London Press* for her expertise and ability to help create something special in every book her publishing company produces. I truly value her advice on the publishing industry.

RECOMMENDED READING

James Alison (2018) The Tablet. *Homosexuality Amongst the Clergy: Caught in a Trap of Dishonesty:* (August edition)

Sue Atkinson (2006) *Breaking the Chains of Abuse:* Lion Hudson plc

Gareth Byrne (2017) *Love One Another as I have Loved You:* Veritas Publications

Donald B. Cozzens (2000) *The Changing Face of the Priesthood:* The Liturgical Press

Brian Davies (1993) *The Thought of Thomas Aquinas:* Clarendon Press

Jim Deeds and Brendan McManus (2017) *Finding God in the Mess: Meditations for Mindful Living:* Messenger Publications

Bill Donohue (2019) *Common Sense Catholicism — How to Resolve Our Cultural Crisis:* Ignatius Press

Bill Donohue (2013) *Why Catholicism Matters:* Image Publications

Mark Dowd (2017) *Queer and Catholic: A Life of Contradiction:* Darton, Longman and Todd Ltd

Kevin Egan (2011) *Remaining a Catholic After the Murphy Report:* Columba Press

Margaret A. Farley (2008) *Just Love: A Framework for Christian Sexual Ethics:* Continuum

Tony Flannery (2013) *A Question of Conscience:* Londubh Books

Tony Flannery (1999) *From the Inside: A Priest's View of the Catholic Church:* The Mercier Press Ltd

Susan Gately (2012) *God Surprise — The New Movements in the Church:* Veritas Publications

Jean-Marie Gueullette (2018) How *to sit with God — A Practical Guide to Silent Prayer:* Veritas Publications

Scott W. Hann (2014) *Evangelizing Catholics — A Mission Manual for the New Evangelization:* Our Sunday Visitor Inc Publications

Tony Hanna (2013) *Dear James Anthony — Why I want to be a Catholic:* Veritas Publications

Leslie Houlden (2003) *Jesus in History Thought and Culture — An Encyclopaedia:* ABC Publications

Gerry O'Hanlon (2018) *The Quiet Revolution of Pope Francis — A Synod Catholic Church in Ireland?:* Messenger Publications

Marie Keenan (2011) *Child Sexual Abuse and the Catholic Church — Gender, Power, and Organizational Culture:* Oxford University Press

Kevin T.Kelly (1998) *New Directions in Sexual Ethics — Moral Theology and the Challenge of AIDS:* Geoffrey Chapman Publishers

Matthew Kelly (2015) *Rediscover Catholicism:* Dynamic Catholic Institute

R.T. Kendall (2009) *Did They think to Pray:* Hodder & Stoughton

Mary Kenny (2000) *Goodbye to Catholic Ireland:* New Island Books

Matthew Linn et al. (1997) *Don't Forgive Too Soon: Extending the Two Hands That Heal:* Paulist Press

Bernard J. Lynch (2012) *If it Wasn't Love: Sex, Death and God:* Circle Books

Mary T. Malone (2019) *The Elephant in the Church:* Columba Books

Briege McKenna (1998) *Miracles Do Happen:* Veritas Publications

James Martin (2018) *Building a Bridge (How the Catholic Church and the LGBT Community Can Enter a Relationship of Respect, Compassion, and Sensitivity):* HarperOne

Frédéric Martel (2019) In the Closet of the Vatican — Power, Homosexuality, Hypocrisy: Bloomsbury

Sean McDonagh (2018) *Laudato Si — An Irish Response: Essays on the Pope's Letter on the Environment:* Veritas Publications

Joe McDonald (2017) *Why the Irish Church Deserves to Die:* Columba Press

Colm O'Gorman (2010) *Beyond Belief: Abused by His Priest:* Hodder & Stoughton

Joseph Ratzinger (1987) *Principles of Catholic Theology:* Ignatius Press

James Bryan Smith (2015) *Hidden in Christ: Living as God's Beloved:* Hodder & Stoughton

Sister Stan (2015) *To Live from the Heart:* Transworld Ireland

Paul Vallely (2013) *Pope Francis: Untying the Knots:* Bloomsbury

Patricia Wittberg (2016) *Catholic Cultures:* Liturgical Press

AUTHOR'S PROFILE

Declan Henry is a creative non-fiction writer with a Master of Science degree in Mental Health Social Work and a Bachelor of Arts (Hons) degree in Education and Community Studies. Declan is a registered social worker and has worked in the profession since 1993. He has written six books and his articles have been widely published in magazines and newspapers. Declan is also a reviewer for the *New York Journal of Books*. He was born in Ballymote, Co Sligo and now lives in Kent. www.declanhenry.co.uk